Encyclopedia
of Transportation

Volume 5

Macmillan Reference USA/An Imprint of The Gale Group
New York

Developed for Macmillan Library Reference USA by
Visual Education Corporation, Princeton, NJ.

For Macmillan

Publisher: Elly Dickason

Senior Editor: Hélène G. Potter

Cover Design: Judy Kahn

For Visual Education

Project Director: Darryl Kestler

Writers: John Haley, Charles Roebuck,
Rebecca Stefoff, Bruce Wetterau

Editors: Cindy George, Doriann Markey,
Charles Roebuck

Associate Editor: Eleanor Hero

Copyediting Manager: Maureen Pancza

Indexer: Sallie Steele

Production Supervisor: Anita Crandall

Design: Maxson Crandall

Electronic Preparation: Cynthia C. Feldner,
Fiona Torphy

Electronic Production: Rob Ehlers,
Lisa Evans-Skopas, Isabelle Ulsh

Macmillan Reference USA
1633 Broadway
New York, NY 10019

PRINTED IN THE UNITED STATES OF AMERICA
1 2 3 4 5 6 7 8 9 10

Library of Congress Cataloging-in-Publication Data

Encyclopedia of transportation.
    p.   cm.
    "Editorial board: Enoch J. Durbin . . . [et al.]"--v. 1, p.   .
    Includes bibliographical references and index.
    Summary: An encyclopedia covering different methods
of transportation and key events, people, and social, economic, and political issues in the history of transportation.
    ISBN 0-02-865361-0 (6 vol. set)
    1. Transportation Encyclopedias.   [1. Transportation
Encyclopedias.] I. Durbin, Enoch.   II. Macmillan Reference USA.
    HE141.E53   1999
    388´.03--dc21   99-33371
                                                                      CIP

Sailing

Sailing is a popular recreation and sport enjoyed by people around the world. For many years, before the age of steam, it was also a necessary skill for trade and travel by ship. Sailing combines a sense of adventure with the pleasure of traveling on a river, lake, or ocean under the power of the wind. Enthusiasts find satisfaction in using their skills to handle their boat and its sails in a variety of wind, weather, and water conditions.

Harnessing the Wind. Sailing depends on the power of the wind. By capturing the wind's energy, the sails propel the boat through the water. When a sailboat is heading in the same direction as the wind (with the wind coming from behind), the force of the wind pushes against the back of the sails, moving the boat forward. Often, however, a boat must sail against the wind to advance toward a destination.

A sailboat can travel at an angle to the wind but not directly into the wind. When the boat moves at an angle to the wind, some of the air striking the sail pushes against the side facing the wind. Some air also blows across the outer curved side of the sail that is filled with wind. This process creates **lift,** the same force that pushes up the wings of an airplane enabling it to fly. In sailing, however, the force of the lift pulls the boat forward instead of upward because the sail is mounted vertically.

lift *force that pushes an aircraft (or other body) up and keeps it airborne*

Controlling Direction. The rudder and keel of a sailboat play an important part in controlling its direction. The rudder is a steering device located at the rear, or stern, of the boat. The keel is a piece of metal, usually V-shaped, that extends downward from the bottom of the boat. Instead of a keel, some small boats have a centerboard, a finlike piece of wood or metal that can be raised or lowered into the water below the boat.

Turning the sailboat's rudder to one side or the other points the front, or bow, of the boat in the desired direction. This is important for positioning the sails to catch the wind, as well as for keeping the boat headed toward a particular destination.

Sailing has become a popular recreation and sport enjoyed by people around the world.

maneuver series of changes in course

The keel or centerboard stops the boat from being pushed sideways when sailing at an angle to the wind. All boats slip somewhat, but keels and centerboards provide resistance that reduces this movement. They also help keep sailboats from leaning over too far in strong winds.

Sailing Maneuvers. There are three basic **maneuvers** in sailing: running, reaching, and beating. Using these operations a person can sail in any direction, except directly into the wind.

In running—also called sailing before the wind—the wind comes directly over the stern of the boat, which travels in the same direction as the wind is blowing. The sails are set nearly perpendicular—at a right angle—to the keel to capture as much wind as possible. It might seem that running would be the fastest type of sailing, but it is generally slower than reaching because the wind only pushes against the back of the sails, and no air flows across the front of them to create lift. Sometimes a large, billowing sail called a spinnaker is set at the front of the boat to gain additional speed.

In reaching—also called sailing across the wind—the air is blowing across the side of the boat, which sails away from the wind at an angle to it. The sails are positioned at an angle to capture as much wind as possible. Sailboats travel fastest while reaching because of the lift produced by the position of the sails.

Beating—also called sailing into the wind—is when the wind is blowing at an angle across the bow of the sailboat. Sailboats can sail into the wind only up to an angle of about 45 degrees. If the boat points more directly into the wind, its sails start to flap, or luff, and they lose the force of the wind.

Sailboats usually follow a zigzag course called tacking, which takes them back and forth across the direction of the wind. Used along with the three basic sailing maneuvers, tacking allows sailboats to travel toward any destination. In changing tacks, the sails are shifted from one side to another to catch the wind. Tacking with the wind coming from behind the boat is known as jibing. This can be a dangerous sailing maneuver if not done properly.

Performing these maneuvers and gaining the best advantage of the winds requires adjusting the sails by pulling them in or letting them out, a procedure called trimming the sails. To trim the sails properly, a sailor must always be aware of the direction of the wind. Sailors trim the sails with ropes called sheets.

One other sailing maneuver is worth mentioning—stopping a sailboat. This can be done by simply turning the boat directly into the wind so that the sails luff. Lowering the sails will also stop the boat, but it takes longer and the boat will continue gliding across the water for a short time.

Seamanship. Sailing involves more than just knowing basic maneuvers and performing them. It also involves seamanship—the knowledge and skills needed to operate a boat safely. As with any other type of vehicle, sailors must follow various rules that govern their movements in relation to other boats. Based on the International Rules of the Road at Sea—a series of regulations originally designed for commercial

Solo Voyages

Completing a voyage around the world by sailboat is challenging enough, but doing it alone is almost unimaginable. Just finding the way across thousands of miles of ocean requires enormous skill and daring. The lone sailor has full responsibility night and day for steering the boat, raising the sails, and tending the various ropes and other rigging. He or she must also face storms that create towering waves and other unexpected emergencies. Despite the dangers, a few brave individuals have made solo voyages around the world. Sir Francis Chichester, a 65-year-old Englishman, succeeded in 1966–1967. Twenty years later, Philippe Monet of France completed the fastest round-the-world solo trip—129 days and 19 hours.

sailing ships—these rules help direct and control traffic on water. Sailing also requires a knowledge of navigation and various navigational signals, such as **buoys** and lighthouses, as well as the ability to read sailing charts and plot and follow courses over water.

buoy *floating marker in the water*

Sailboat Racing. Competitive racing is a popular sport around the world. Each year sailboats of all types and sizes can participate in thousands of local, national, and international races that test the speed of the boats and the skill of their crews. A series of races called a regatta typically has many entrants.

There are three basic types of sailboat races: one-design races, rating races, and handicap races. One-design races include only boats of the same type and size. Since the boats are all evenly matched, winning these races depends largely on the sailing skills of the crew.

In rating races, the boats are not identical. However, they must all fall within the same approximate rating class. The rating of each boat is calculated according to complicated formulas that include such factors as the length of the boat and the sail area.

Most long-distance and ocean races are handicap races, in which boats of all sizes and types compete against each other. Before such races begin, each boat is rated according to a formula and assigned a handicap, or time allowance, which helps to equalize all the boats in terms of performance and speed. A boat's handicap is deducted from the total time it takes to complete the race, which means that the first boat across the finish line is not necessarily the winner.

Although there are many international sailboat races, the America's Cup is the most famous. Held at intervals since the 1870s, this race was won continuously by American entrants until 1983. Since then the prize has gone in turn to Australian, American, and New Zealand sailboats. *See also* NAVIGATION; SAILBOATS AND SAILING SHIPS; SHIPS AND BOATS, PARTS OF; SHIPS AND BOATS, SAFETY OF; SHIPS AND BOATS, TYPES OF.

St. Lawrence Seaway

An important waterway for commercial shipping in North America, the St. Lawrence Seaway makes it possible for oceangoing vessels to sail directly from the Atlantic Ocean to the Great Lakes. Located along the border between Canada and the United States, the seaway and connecting waterways—including the Great Lakes—extend for 9,500 miles (15,285 km). The seaway itself consists of a 2,350-mile (3,781-km) stretch formed by the St. Lawrence River, lakes, and a network of canals and locks.

Before the seaway was built in 1959, most large vessels could take the St. Lawrence River from the Atlantic Ocean to Montreal, Canada, and from Ogdensburg, New York, to the head of the Great Lakes. However, only small craft were able to pass through the narrow channels of the St. Lawrence between Montreal and Ogdensburg, a distance of 186 miles (299 km).

The first efforts to improve transportation along the river began during the late 1600s when European traders dug canals to bypass rapids near Montreal. Over the following centuries an extensive system of

The St. Lawrence Seaway allows ocean-going vessels to sail directly from the Atlantic Ocean to the Great Lakes. It takes a ship about one and one-half days to travel the entire length of the seaway.

canals and locks was built. By 1903 Canada had created a waterway with a minimum depth of 14 feet (4.3 m) extending from the Gulf of St. Lawrence to Lake Erie. In 1932 the Welland Ship Canal was completed near Niagara Falls, opening a 25-foot (8-m) deep passage between Lake Ontario and Lake Erie that included eight locks. Meanwhile, the United States worked on connecting channels between the Great Lakes. By 1914 ships that could float in less than 21 feet (6 m) of water were able to travel all the way from Lake Erie to the far western side of Lake Superior.

Although a joint Canadian-U.S. project to build a full-fledged waterway for oceangoing ships began in the early 1900s, opposition in the U.S. Congress stalled it for more than 40 years. Finally, in 1954, with the backing of the Eisenhower administration, Congress passed the Wiley-Dondero Act, authorizing the project. Plans included widening and deepening sections of the waterway to a minimum depth of 27 feet (8 m) and a width of 200 feet (61 m), and building three dams and a jointly operated power plant. The St. Lawrence Seaway was formally opened on June 26, 1959.

The enlargement of the river allowed oceangoing cargo ships to carry goods to industrial and agricultural centers in Canada and the American Midwest. Most of the cargo consists of bulk materials such as grain, iron ore, and coal, but automobiles, steel, and other manufactured goods are also transported. It takes about one and one-half days for a ship to travel the entire length of the seaway. Ice closes down the passage from mid-December to early April. *See also* CANALS; PANAMA CANAL.

Salvage

Salvage is the rescue of a ship or cargo at risk of being lost or destroyed. Salvors, as the rescuers are called, also recover vessels that have sunk or have been abandoned.

Salvage Operations. The primary function of a salvage operation is to tow disabled ships to port for repairs. An engine malfunction,

A salvage diver works on the wreck of the Mecca, a freighter that sank in the Suez Canal in 1967.

a fire, or the loss of steering can leave a vessel drifting helplessly at sea and force the ship's owner to call for assistance. Salvage tugs often rescue vessels that have run aground because of storms, poor visibility caused by fog, human error, or failure of the ship's radar or other navigational aids. They may also be hired to recover a vessel that sank after a collision or storm.

One of the largest salvage operations ever undertaken involved raising 44 German battleships that had been sunk off the coast of Scotland during World War I. The most famous salvage operation in recent years is that of the luxury liner *Titanic*. After its wreck was discovered in 1985, numerous expeditions to the site retrieved about 5,000 objects, including a 20-ton section of the ship's outer hull.

The large seaworthy tugs used by salvage companies are typically 150 to 250 feet (46 to 76 m) long and feature engines that range up to 10,000 horsepower. The tugs carry a wide array of equipment: heavy anchors, cables, ropes, chains, patching material, air compressors, pumps, diving gear, fire-fighting tools, blasting machinery, and so on. Crew members include divers, machinists, and pump engineers.

The cost of salvage depends on the services rendered. Salvage companies usually charge a flat fee for a tow to the nearest port. The recovery of a shipwreck or its cargo is generally carried out under contract. Because this type of salvage is expensive, a ship or cargo owner must weigh the value of saving a damaged vessel and its contents against the cost of refloating or restoring it. If a ship has sunk in very deep waters or is badly damaged, the owner may decide to save only the cargo.

Salvage Techniques. In good weather and calm seas, recovering a disabled ship may involve little more than attaching a line between the drifting ship and the salvage tug. Likewise, a ship that has run aground and is not taking on water sometimes can be pulled to deeper water by one or two tugs. High tide may also provide the extra lift needed to release the vessel. In some cases, salvage crews remove cargo and portable equipment to lighten the ship before towing begins. If the salvors still cannot free the ship, they may try using heavy pulleys and cables attached to the grounded ship or, as a last resort, cut the ship in half and tow away the part that can be moved.

Raising a sunken ship is usually the most difficult and dangerous task for a salvage operation. Divers first examine the wreck to decide whether and how it can be recovered. If a decision is made to raise the ship, salvors may use several techniques. One is to attach floats to the ship. The floats are pumped full of air, rise to the surface, and bring the ship up with them. Another approach involves sealing all openings and then filling the ship with compressed air. The air forces the water out and causes the ship to rise to the surface. *See also* Accidents; Maritime Hazards; Maritime Law.

Salyut Space Stations

Soviet Union *nation that existed from 1922 to 1991, made up of Russia and 14 other republics in eastern Europe and northern Asia*

cosmonaut *Russian term for a person who travels into space; literally, "traveler to the universe"*

The Soviet Union launched a series of space stations called Salyut during the 1970s and 1980s.

Salyut was the name given to a series of space stations operated by the **Soviet Union** for civilian and military purposes during the 1970s and 1980s. *Salyut 1*, launched on April 19, 1971, was the world's first working space station. Made up of a number of cylinder-shaped sections of different sizes, the station measured nearly 50 feet (15 m) long and 13 feet (4 m) wide and could carry a crew of three **cosmonauts.** Four solar panels supplied power to *Salyut 1*, and a docking port allowed one piloted Soyuz spacecraft to link up with the station.

The Salyut program had early difficulties. The first cosmonauts who docked at *Salyut 1* were not able to enter it. The second crew spent more than three weeks in the station. Unfortunately, during the cosmonauts'

return to Earth, the oxygen supply leaked out of their Soyuz spacecraft, killing all three men. *Salyut 2* fell out of orbit soon after its launch in April 1973 and was never occupied. The next three Salyut stations enjoyed some success, with crews establishing records for length of time in space. The cosmonauts returned to Earth, and eventually the stations fell out of orbit and burned up in the atmosphere.

Salyut 6 and *Salyut 7,* launched in 1977 and 1982, achieved the greatest success, mainly because they were redesigned to have two docking ports. This change allowed the stations to be resupplied by unpiloted spacecraft, enabling the crew to make repairs and greatly extending the length of time they could remain on board. In 1984 the crew of *Salyut 7* set a record of 237 days in space. The last crew to visit the station left in March 1986, and *Salyut 7* fell back into Earth's atmosphere in 1991. *See also* Mir; Skylab; Soyuz Spacecraft; Space Exploration; Space Rovers; Space Stations; Space Travel.

Santa Fe Trail

Perils of the Trail

The Sante Fe Trail crossed raging rivers, mountain passes, and parched deserts. Merchants leading wagon trains loaded with goods braved these hazards to carry their goods to the markets of New Mexico. At the Arkansas River, drivers had to decide whether to float their wagons across or to take their chances with patches of quicksand in the river's shallow stretches. The western branch of the trail led over the high Raton Mountains, where traders used ropes to lower their wagons down the sheer slopes. The eastern route along the Cimarron Cutoff was just as treacherous. Here, the wagons had to cross 50 miles of desert sand to reach Santa Fe.

tributary *stream or river that flows into a larger stream or river*

An important trading route in the American Southwest from 1821 to 1880, the Santa Fe Trail extended 780 miles (1,255 km) between Missouri and New Mexico. Merchants typically traveled along the trail in large wagon trains, which carried manufactured goods to Santa Fe and returned east loaded with silver, mules, and furs.

Origin of the Trail. In the early 1800s, Santa Fe was a northern outpost of the Spanish colony of Mexico. The Spanish refused to allow Americans to trade with this town. The situation changed in 1821 when Mexico won its independence from Spain. On hearing the news of the new government, American trader William Becknell immediately set out for Santa Fe with a small group of men and pack mules. Upon reaching the city, he found a ready market for his manufactured goods and traded them for a fortune in silver.

Returning the following year with a wagon train, Becknell established what would become the main route of the Santa Fe Trail. Starting in Franklin, Missouri, he traveled westward along the divide between the **tributaries** of the Kansas and Arkansas Rivers. At what is now Great Bend, Kansas, Becknell followed the Arkansas River for about 100 miles (161 km). Then taking advantage of a shallow crossing near present-day Cimarron, Kansas, he headed directly southwest to Santa Fe.

Becknell's route, known as the Cimarron Cutoff, was quick but dangerous. It crossed the desert, where water was scarce and Comanche Indians sometimes attacked the wagon trains. The Mountain Branch, a longer route, followed the Arkansas River westward for another 150 miles (241 km) to Bent's Fort, then crossed the Arkansas River and headed southwest over the Raton Mountains to Santa Fe.

The Golden Years. Trade over the Santa Fe Trail grew steadily. Between the 1820s and 1840s, an average of 80 wagons and 150 people traveled the route each year. Wagon trains moved westward in parallel columns as a precaution against attacks by Native Americans. At the first sign of trouble, the wagons would quickly form a circle, which could be defended more easily.

As trading activity on the Santa Fe Trail expanded, so did profits, and an increasing number of Americans settled in the region. The American victory in the war with Mexico (1846–1848) brought Santa Fe and the trail leading to it entirely within U.S. borders.

The California gold rush created another surge in traffic on the trail. Some 12,000 people used it in 1848 and 1849 on their way to California. The start of regular stagecoach mail service and the westward expansion of the United States made the Santa Fe Trail one of the most famous and long-lasting wagon roads of the American West. It remained in regular use until the Atchison, Topeka, and Santa Fe Railroad was completed in 1880, since the railroad followed a route similar to that of the trail. *See also* OREGON TRAIL; ROADS.

Satellites

A satellite is an artificial object orbiting the Earth. Satellites perform many useful functions ranging from communication transmission and scientific research, to providing information on weather and navigation, to spying. There are more than 2,000 satellites in orbit around Earth.

Brief History

"The Brick Moon," a story written by Edward Everett Hale in 1869, mentions placing an artificial satellite in space. Nearly 90 years passed before this bit of science fiction became reality with the flight of the **Soviet Union**'s *Sputnik 1* on October 4, 1957. *Sputnik 1* carried only two radio transmitters and no instruments for scientific measurements. However, it amazed the world and made history as the first artificial satellite.

American scientists responded quickly, but their initial program to put a satellite in space, called Vanguard, failed. In January 1958, however, the United States succeeded in launching *Explorer 1,* the first of many Explorer satellites sent into orbit. *Explorer 1* discovered an intense zone of **radiation** surrounding the Earth that was later named the Van Allen radiation belts.

Since that time, thousands of satellites have been placed in space. Most nonmilitary American satellites have been launched by the National Aeronautics and Space Administration (NASA), a government agency established in 1958 to manage the nation's space programs. The U.S. Air Force has launched most military satellites. The Soviet—and then the Russian—space program also continued to send satellites into orbit for exploration, communications, weather forecasting, and scientific research.

The era of commercial communications satellites began in 1962 with the launch of *Telstar,* which was owned by a phone company. International cooperation got under way in 1964, when several countries established INTELSAT, a worldwide communications satellite network. INTELSAT now includes more than 130 member nations. In the 1970s a number of nations began to produce satellites. Most of these were launched by either the United States or the Soviet Union.

Soviet Union *nation that existed from 1922 to 1991, made up of Russia and 14 other republics in eastern Europe and northern Asia*

radiation *energy given off in waves or particles*

Further Information
To learn more about satellites, including communication and navigation satellites and the use of satellites in space exploration, see the related articles listed at the end of this entry.

In 1975 a group of eight nations in Western Europe formed the European Space Agency (ESA) to create and launch satellites. China, Japan, Israel, India, Brazil, and several other nations have also placed satellites in orbit.

Satellites and Their Orbits

probe *uncrewed spacecraft sent out to explore and collect information in space*

Satellites are classified mainly by orbit and function. While space **probes** are designed to leave Earth's orbit and explore the solar system, satellites circle the Earth and perform specific tasks. The function of a satellite largely determines its design and its orbit.

Satellite Orbits. Satellites move around Earth in a variety of orbits. Some are circular; others are elliptical, or oval-shaped. The altitude of orbits also differs, ranging from about 155 miles (250 km) to over 20,000 miles (32,180 km). Most satellites travel in a low-altitude orbit, a geosynchronous orbit, or a sun-synchronous polar orbit.

A satellite in a low-altitude orbit follows a circular path in the uppermost layers of Earth's atmosphere. Launching a satellite into this type of

Landsat satellites photograph regions of the Earth and study the effects of human activity on the environment. This photo shows a map of the barren terrain of Death Valley in southern California.

orbit requires less energy than sending one further into space. Large research satellites, such as the Hubble Space Telescope, are usually placed in low-altitude orbit.

A satellite in a geosynchronous orbit moves in the same direction and speed as Earth's rotation on its axis. This allows the satellite to remain above the same point on Earth at all times, an essential condition for communications satellites that receive and transmit signals from fixed points on Earth.

A sun-synchronous polar orbit is one in which a satellite travels over the Earth's poles. The satellite passes over different parts of the planet, but its movement is coordinated so that it always crosses the equator at the same time. This type of orbit allows a satellite to observe and compare data from the same area on Earth at the same time each day over a period of days, weeks, or longer. It is extremely useful for weather satellites and various Earth-observing satellites.

Types of Satellites. Satellites are designed for specific purposes. Research satellites gather scientific data. Some, such as the Landsat series of satellites, photograph and map the Earth and study the effects of human activity on the environment. Others measure the Earth's gravitational field and radiation. Astronomical satellites, such as the Orbiting Solar Observatories launched in the 1960s and the Hubble Space Telescope launched in 1990, observe the Sun, stars, planets, and other objects in space.

Communications satellites receive and transmit telephone, television, radio, fax, and other telecommunications signals from around the world. A single satellite can relay thousands of telephone calls and hundreds of television channels at once. *Echo 1*, one of the earliest communications satellites, was launched by NASA in 1960. Most modern communications satellites are owned and operated by private companies.

Weather satellites are used to identify and predict developing weather patterns. They also gather information on temperature, precipitation, and winds. Satellites placed in geosynchronous orbits can monitor the weather over the same region of the world at all times. Those in sun-synchronous polar orbits can observe and compare weather conditions over the entire planet. *Tiros 1*, launched by NASA in 1960, was the world's first weather satellite.

Navigation satellites, such as those that make up the Global Positioning System, help pilots, ship captains, and people traveling on land determine their position. Vehicles equipped for satellite navigation receive radio signals from several satellites, and a computer analyzes the signals and calculates the location of the vehicle to within 100 feet (30 m). Navigation satellites move in geosynchronous orbits because they must be anchored to reference points on Earth to provide accurate navigational data.

The military relies on top-secret **reconnaissance** and electronic intelligence satellites to photograph military installations, to observe and track the movement of troops and equipment, and to monitor foreign communications. Many Earth-observing satellites—including those involved in research, reconnaissance, and weather studies—follow sun-synchronous

Eye in the Sky

Military spy satellites have been taking pictures of Earth since 1960. *Discoverer 14,* the first successful U.S. spy satellite, could photograph objects on Earth as small as 1 foot (0.3 m). Film from the early satellites was ejected in a capsule and grabbed in the air by an airplane. Then, in 1976, the United States launched the *KH-11* satellite, which transmits images from onboard telescopes and video cameras directly to ground stations. Some sources say the *KH-11* can identify objects as small as 6 inches (15 cm) from thousands of miles in space.

reconnaissance act of searching, inspecting, and observing for the purpose of gaining information

polar orbits because this type of orbit allows them to gather data almost anywhere in the world. *See also* EUROPEAN SPACE AGENCY; GLOBAL POSITIONING SYSTEM (GPS); INTELSAT; NASA; SPACECRAFT, PARTS OF; SPACE EXPLORATION; SPACE PROBES; SPUTNIK 1.

Schooners

In the 1700s and 1800s, schooners were the main sailing ships used for trade and fishing. These vessels dominated North American waters until the introduction of the speedy clipper ships in the mid-1800s.

Schooners feature two or more masts and sails rigged fore-and-aft—stretched toward the bow and the stern—of each mast. One or more of these sails are jibs, triangular sails located between the mainmast and the bow. Andrew Robinson, a shipbuilder from Massachusetts, built the first schooner in 1713. Early schooners usually had just two masts, a tall mainmast in the stern and a slightly smaller foremast in the bow. Later designs included as many as six masts.

maneuverable *able to make a series of changes in course easily*

square-rigged *having rectangular sails*

Fast and **maneuverable** in shallow waters, schooners were well suited to coastal sailing. They handled the unpredictable wind patterns of coastal areas better than **square-rigged** ships. Schooners also required smaller crews than square-rigged vessels of comparable size.

In the mid-1800s schooners inspired the development of the famous clipper ships. By the 1920s the great schooners had been largely replaced by steamships. Today the schooner design survives in large two-masted pleasure yachts. *See also* CARGO SHIPS; CLIPPER SHIPS; SAILBOATS AND SAILING SHIPS; YACHTS.

Sea Chanteys

see Songs.

Seaplanes

Seaplanes are aircraft that can take off, land, and float on water. They are particularly useful in remote areas that lack appropriate terrain for runways but have calm bodies of water nearby.

There are two main types of seaplanes: flying boats and float planes. Flying boats feature watertight hulls that possess enough **buoyancy** and strength to allow them to float and land on water. Two small pontoons, or floats, located beneath the wings help to stabilize the aircraft and prevent the wings from dipping beneath the water.

buoyancy *force that exerts an upward push on an object*

Float planes are standard aircraft to which two or more pontoons have been attached to make them suitable for use on water. A less common type of seaplane is an amphibian, which has retractable wheels mounted on its floats or hull. The pilot can move the wheels up or down, making the aircraft **amphibious.**

amphibious *able to move on land and through water*

The first practical seaplanes were built and flown in 1911 by American aviator Glenn Curtiss. During World War I, British seaplanes called F-boats engaged in antisubmarine warfare and carried out ocean patrols and air-sea rescue missions. After the war, a U.S. Navy seaplane crossed the North Atlantic Ocean, setting a long-distance flying record.

Seaplanes, which can take off and land on bodies of water, are used mostly for sport and recreational flying.

Seaplanes progressed rapidly during the 1920s, and for a time they were the largest and fastest aircraft in the world. Multiengine flying boats pioneered commercial air travel in the 1930s, carrying passengers between such cities as Moscow and New York and Rome and Rio de Janeiro.

Although seaplanes continued to play a critical role in military operations during World War II, their importance began to decline soon after the war. Manufacturers developed standard aircraft that could fly long distances as well as aircraft carriers. The construction of more landing fields and airports around the world further reduced the need for seaplanes.

The development of seaplanes has continued but only on a very small scale. Today most of them are small single-engine float planes used for sport or recreational flying. In some remote areas, such as parts of Alaska, seaplanes provide passenger transportation between isolated communities. *See also* AIRCRAFT; AIRCRAFT, MILITARY; AIRLINE INDUSTRY; AIRPORTS; AVIATION, HISTORY OF; CURTISS, GLENN.

Sedan Chairs

A sedan chair was a one-person vehicle that consisted of a chair placed inside a closed compartment with side windows. The passenger entered through a door in the front of the compartment. Two men—one in front of the compartment and one behind—stood between two long horizontal poles attached to the sides of the vehicle. They raised the sedan chair and carried the passenger to a destination. Another version of the sedan chair had wheels and required only one person to pull it.

The ancient Assyrians and Persians of the Middle East used sedan chairs. In the 1600s the vehicles began to appear in Europe, probably spreading from Italy to London and other cities. Because sedan chairs took up less road space than horse-drawn coaches, they helped to relieve traffic on city streets. Well-to-do Americans in the urban centers of New York and Philadelphia also used sedan chairs in colonial times. Some of these vehicles were privately owned and elaborately decorated; others operated for hire. After the early 1800s, the sedan chair disappeared from American and European cities but remained for a while in Asia. *See also* CARTS, CARRIAGES, AND WAGONS.

Service Stations

Motor vehicles require fuel, maintenance, and from time to time, repair. Drivers can obtain the necessary products and services at the thousands of service stations—gas stations—located along streets, roads, and highways in the United States and elsewhere.

The earliest service station dedicated to selling gasoline for automobiles opened in Bordeaux, France, in 1896. Since that time, service stations have become an essential part of the transportation industry worldwide.

The majority of gas stations offer gasoline, oil, and diesel fuel, but maintenance and repair services vary. Some places provide only routine services, such as changing oil or fixing a flat tire. Others, often called garages, specialize in engine tune-ups, auto body work, and major repairs. Most stations are equipped with public bathrooms and telephones, and some even have convenience stores.

The level of service available generally depends on the personnel at the service station and its location. Some stations employ attendants who only refuel motor vehicles; those that offer automotive repair and maintenance have qualified mechanics on staff. In some states, stations

Besides selling gasoline and changing oil, many service stations have mechanics on duty to inspect and repair vehicles.

are self-serve—drivers pump their own gasoline or diesel fuel and pay a cashier. *See also* AUTOMOBILES: RELATED INDUSTRIES; ENERGY; ENGINES.

Shepard, Alan
American astronaut

NASA *National Aeronautics and Space Administration, the U.S. space agency*

cosmonaut *Russian term for a person who travels into space; literally, "traveler to the universe"*

Alan B. Shepard, Jr., was the first American astronaut to travel in space. Born in 1923, Shepard began his military career with the U.S. Navy in 1944 and served in the Pacific Ocean during World War II. He later entered flight training and became a military test pilot. In 1959 **NASA** chose Shepard as one of seven pilots in the first astronaut corps.

On May 5, 1961, about one month after the Soviet Union sent **cosmonaut** Yuri Gagarin into space, NASA launched a Mercury capsule named *Freedom 7*, with Shepard aboard, from Cape Canaveral, Florida. Shepard's 15-minute flight followed an arc that passed through the upper atmosphere at an altitude of 117 miles (188 km) and ended in the Atlantic Ocean 302 miles (486 km) east of Florida. The mission did not match Gagarin's orbit of the Earth, but its success boosted U.S. morale as the country struggled to compete with the Soviet space program.

In 1971 Shepard commanded *Apollo 14*, a mission that landed on the Fra Mauro highlands of the Moon, where he and Edgar D. Mitchell conducted geological experiments. Shepard retired to a career in private business in 1975 and died in 1998. *See also* APOLLO PROGRAM; GAGARIN, YURI; SPACE EXPLORATION.

Shipbuilding

From the reed boats of the ancient Egyptians to the gigantic steel supertankers of today, shipbuilders have produced an amazing array of vessels. Making ships strong enough to survive the pounding of wind and waves has always been a prime concern of shipbuilders. Many other factors also influence the design and construction of ships.

History of Shipbuilding

Throughout history, shipbuilders have had to deal with certain basic problems. Perhaps the most crucial is constructing a hull that will stay afloat—even when the ship is heavily loaded—and not sag at the ends when the ship goes over large waves (called hogging).

The Ancient World. The ancient Egyptians solved the problem of hogging by running a thick rope from the bow of their reed ships, over the top of the mast, and back down to the stern. As time went on, shipbuilders learned how to make stronger hulls and larger ships. The Phoenicians and Greeks constructed hulls of heavy planks laid over an internal frame. Their solid ships, powered by sails and oars, could undertake long voyages across the Mediterranean and even into the Atlantic Ocean.

The Romans raised shipbuilding to a new level. Their ships had wide round-ended hulls with a massive framework of wooden planks and crosspieces. Large Roman merchant ships could carry 400 tons of cargo and ranged up to 180 feet (55 m) long and 45 feet (14 m) wide. Roman warships were even larger, measuring up to 235 feet (72 m) long and 110 feet (34 m) wide.

Rise of Modern Shipbuilding.

In the 1400s the Portuguese and the Spanish built sturdy sailing ships with deep hulls made of wooden planks laid edge to edge (called caravel construction). These ships became the standard for European shipbuilding.

Meanwhile, changes in naval warfare led to developments in ship design. The use of cannons brought new concerns. For one, the extra weight of heavy cannons increased the instability of the vessel in rough water. Furthermore, cannon fire placed great stress on the ship's structure. Shipbuilders solved these problems, in part, by making the topsides of ships curve inward and placing extra bracing and stronger joints in the hull.

By the late 1500s another change in shipbuilding was under way. Up to that time, shipbuilders had relied on their "eye" and rule-of-thumb methods instead of drawn plans. But the need for stronger, more complex construction forced the builders to design ships on paper before making them. Experts in drawing plans for ships became known as naval architects.

The introduction of iron hulls in the mid-1800s revolutionized shipbuilding. The *Great Britain,* the first oceangoing iron ship, was launched in 1843. Its iron hull—fortified by iron beams running lengthwise—had an inner and outer bottom as well as crosswise bulkheads, or partitions. The bulkheads added strength and created watertight compartments inside the hull.

Two other important advances in shipbuilding occurred in the late 1800s. Steel replaced iron in ships, and scale-model testing led to improvements in the science of hull design. Since then, models of new ship designs are routinely tested in water tanks before construction begins.

Shipbuilding Today

Building modern ships is a complex and costly process. Naval architects and shipbuilders must consider many factors, including the purpose of the vessel, where it will be used, how fast it must travel, the type of cargo it will carry, and meeting certain safety requirements. What the ship will be made of—steel, wood, or other material—and how it will be powered—by steam engines, diesel engines, or sails—are other important considerations.

Design, Planning, and Construction.

All large ships today are built according to plans drawn by naval architects. The architect makes small-scale drawings of the proposed vessel and prepares estimates of such things as cargo capacity, the size of the ship's engines, and fuel consumption under normal conditions. These drawings and estimates are presented to the shipowner for approval.

The Ship That Did Not Want to Launch

Constructed in England in 1853, the *Great Eastern* was 692 feet (211 m) long—the longest ship built up to that time. Because of its size, the ship's builders faced many design problems and huge cost overruns. Furthermore, the great length of the ship meant that its launching into the Thames River would have to be sideways. When launch day arrived, the mighty ship moved a few inches on the launching ramp and then became stuck. Workers built special rams to push the *Great Eastern* down the ramp and set up giant winches on the opposite bank of the river to pull the ship as well. The preparations took weeks. On the next attempt the river was at high tide, and the trouble-plagued ship finally slid down the ramp into the water.

At this shipyard in the Netherlands, workers construct the framework for the hull of a wooden sailing ship.

keel *wood or metal structure that runs lengthwise along the bottom of a boat and helps strengthen it*

Using the architect's plans, specialists at the shipyard prepare large-scale working diagrams. These detailed drawings show the various parts of the ship, provide precise measurements and dimensions, and indicate how the parts fit together. In traditional shipbuilding, workers also used full-scale templates, or patterns, to build and shape the pieces of the ship. Computerization has eliminated the need for many such drawings.

While readying the diagrams and templates, shipyard workers determine the sequence in which the parts of the ship will be built and prepare a work schedule to ensure timely completion of the vessel. Some parts, such as steel hull plates and propeller shafts, must be ordered from manufacturers.

Most ships today are not built piece by piece from the **keel** up as they were in the past. Instead, large sections of the hull are constructed at the same time in different parts of the shipyard. The completed sections are then transported to an area called the building berth, where they are positioned and welded into place.

Once the hull has been welded together, preassembled sections of the superstructure—structures above the ship's main deck—are lowered into place on the ship and welded fast. Many of these sections already have electrical wiring and piping installed, which speeds up the finishing stages later on.

Launching and Outfitting. When the hull is finished and most other parts are in place, the ship is ready for launching. Ships can be set into the water stern first, sideways, or by floating them off the assembly area. Most ships are launched with the vessel sliding stern first down a ramp into the water. Launching is usually a tense time because a ship can be damaged if it does not slide properly down the ramp into the water.

After launching, the ship is towed to another part of the shipyard for final outfitting—the process of installing the remaining equipment needed to operate the ship. This includes navigational equipment, electrical and plumbing systems, interior furnishings, deck fittings, and final coats of paint. When outfitting is complete, the ship undergoes a series of tests, called trials, to make sure that all its equipment is operating properly and that the vessel performs according to the architect's plan.

Traditional Shipbuilding. All large ships are built this way, but traditional shipbuilding methods are often used for wooden yachts and small boats. This generally means constructing the boat from bottom to top—laying the keel first, shaping and attaching the pieces that make up the framework of the hull, fastening planking to the hull, putting in decking, and building the upper portions of the vessel. *See also* SAILBOATS AND SAILING SHIPS; SHIPS AND BOATS; SHIPS AND BOATS, PARTS OF; SHIPS AND BOATS, TYPES OF.

Shipping Industry

For thousands of years, most of the goods that have been transported over long distances have made their journey by ship. Even though jet airplanes can now cross the oceans in a matter of hours, the world's **merchant marine** still carries the great majority of overseas cargo. As a result, shipping is one of the largest and most important industries in the world.

merchant marine vessels engaged in commerce; officers and crews of such vessels

History of the Shipping Industry

Humans have been transporting goods by water ever since they first used rafts. As early civilizations expanded, people began to exchange items with more distant communities. Traders realized that transporting their goods by sea was faster and easier than hauling them over land.

Ancient and Medieval Shipping. The Phoenicians, who dominated shipping in the Mediterranean Sea from about 1200 to 300 B.C., were the first great sea traders. From ports on the eastern Mediterranean they traded with people as far away as Spain and North Africa. The shipment of goods by sea became even more widespread in the Roman Empire. Great ships more than 150 feet (46 m) long transported grain regularly from Egypt to Rome.

Huge cranes are used to load and un-load cargo ships in modern ports such as Hong Kong, shown here.

In northern Europe, the Vikings used wide cargo ships for trade between A.D. 700 and 1000. During the Middle Ages, the Italian cities of Venice and Genoa built large fleets of ships that carried goods between Europe and the Middle East. At about this time, **maritime** insurance was developed to reduce the financial risks of losing ships or cargo at sea.

maritime related to the sea or shipping

The Age of Sail. In the early 1500s, European trading ships began sailing new water routes to Asia. Larger and faster ships were designed to carry cargo on long-distance journeys. After several European nations founded colonies in the Americas, **transatlantic** shipping routes became an important part of international trade. For hundreds of years, Britain, Spain, France, and Holland dominated these routes. After the American Revolution, the United States developed its own shipping industry. By the late 1800s, it had one of the largest merchant fleets in the world.

transatlantic relating to crossing the Atlantic Ocean

In the 1830s shippers began to offer **packet** service, which promised regular sailings between ports. Before this time, a ship usually only sailed if it had a full cargo. The development of packet service made shipping cheaper and more efficient. By the late 1800s, steamships began to replace sailing vessels on the major trade routes.

packet small, fast ship used during the 1800s to carry mail, cargo, and passengers

The Modern Era. During the 1900s cargo ships became larger and faster, and shipping services improved their efficiency. Today, specialized ships are used to transport various types of cargo. Tankers carry liquids, and dry bulk carriers haul loose cargo such as grain or iron ore. Container ships are loaded with boxlike containers filled with freight. Roll-on/roll-off ships transport motor vehicles and wheeled containers that are rolled aboard. LASH (lighter aboard ship) ships haul loaded barges known as lighters.

These specialized ships can be loaded and unloaded quickly. In addition, they can operate with fewer crew members than earlier vessels. Both advanced loading methods and smaller crews reduce shipping costs.

Organization of the Shipping Industry

Shipping companies offer customers a variety of services. Their fees depend on a number of factors, such as the type of cargo, the destination, and the delivery schedule.

Types of Services. The main types of shipping services are liners, tramps, and industrial or captive fleets. Liners carry cargo between particular ports on a regular schedule. Customers can book the service well in advance of the sailing date. This kind of service is particularly useful for companies that ship large quantities of goods along the same routes on a regular basis.

Organizations called conferences set standard rates for goods carried by liner services. They also determine what percentage of the total available shipping can be provided by any one company. The conference system assures that shippers will charge reasonable rates and provide regular service with good vessels and professional crews.

Tramp shippers do not run on fixed schedules or have long-term arrangements with certain companies. Instead, they combine loads of goods from various customers, delivering each shipment to a separate destination. A tramp vessel may travel to many different ports during a single voyage, dropping off and picking up cargo along the way. Tramp shippers sometimes rent ships to customers who are willing to provide their own crew as well as supplies such as food and fuel.

Captive fleets are company ships used for transporting the company's goods. Many oil companies own the large supertankers that carry their oil to refineries and distribution centers. However, operating a shipping fleet is very expensive, and only a few very large corporations have captive fleets. It is usually much cheaper to hire a liner or tramp service for a company's shipping needs.

Today's Merchant Fleets. The world's merchant fleet has grown steadily since the late 1960s. By the late 1990s, it included tens of thousands of ships that could carry a total of more than 700 million tons of goods. Oil tankers and dry bulk carriers made up about 45 percent of the total.

Merchant ships registered in the United States are required to employ American crews. However, shipping industry wages are generally higher in the United States than in some other countries. As a result, many American shipping companies register their vessels in open registry countries—places that have lower taxes, lower labor costs, and fewer safety regulations than the United States. The ships sail under a foreign

Plimsoll Lines

International agreements call for Plimsoll lines to be painted on the hull of every cargo ship. Named for Samuel Plimsoll, a British Member of Parliament who worked for ship safety measures, the lines show how far down in the water a ship may sit when loaded with cargo. The requirements vary, depending on the time of year and the water in which the vessel is sailing. A ship may sit lower in the water in summer than in winter, and lower in fresh water than in salt water. Plimsoll lines help ensure that a ship is not overloaded for the conditions it will encounter on its voyage.

flag, known as a flag of convenience. Most of the ships registered in Panama and Liberia, the two most popular open registry countries, are foreign owned. Russia and China also have large merchant fleets. *See also* BARGES; CANALS; CARGO SHIPS; CHINA TRADE; CLIPPER SHIPS; CONTAINERIZATION; CONVOYS; FREIGHT; HARBORS AND PORTS; INSURANCE; INTERMODAL TRANSPORT; MARITIME LAW; MERCHANT MARINE; REGULATION OF TRANSPORTATION; SHIPBUILDING; SHIPS AND BOATS; SHIPS AND BOATS, TYPES OF; TANKERS; TRADE AND COMMERCE.

Ships and Boats

Further Information
To learn more about ships and boats, including shipbuilding, the shipping industry, navigation, and particular types of vessels, see the related articles listed at the end of this entry.

For thousands of years, ships and boats have transported passengers and goods over the world's oceans, seas, and inland waterways. They remain an important form of transportation, serving as a means of commerce and travel. Today many nations rely on merchant ships to transport raw materials and manufactured goods. Cruise ships and ferries carry passengers between various ports, and naval ships help to defend nations and support military operations.

The distinction between ships and boats is not always clear, though in general boats are smaller cousins of ships. In the age of sail, a ship was a vessel with three masts. Another view holds that a ship is any vessel large enough to carry small boats (such as lifeboats). Another maintains that only large oceangoing craft should be called ships; all other vessels are boats. Although boats may function as a means of transportation, many small vessels are used primarily for recreation and sport.

History of Ships and Boats

The use of ships and boats began in prehistoric times. The earliest vessels were probably crude log rafts that allowed people to cross rivers and lakes. The first true boats may have consisted of animal skins sewn together and stretched over a frame of sticks. From these beginnings, ships and boats became increasingly larger and more complex, leading up to the great sailing ships of the 1700s and 1800s and the freighters, naval vessels, cruise ships, pleasure craft, and other ships and boats of the modern world.

Early Developments. The earliest boats were probably propelled by humans using their hands as paddles. Eventually people developed better means of moving the vessel through water, including wooden paddles, poles for pushing against the bottom in shallow water, and oars—long-handled paddles. By about 4000 B.C. ancient Egyptians had built long, narrow ships driven by a row of oars mounted on each side.

For centuries ships and boats were propelled by oars, by sails, or by a combination of the two. Around 3500 B.C. the Egyptians were making sailboats out of reeds lashed together into bundles. The boats had a single square sail that was used when the wind came from behind the vessel. When there was no wind or when the wind came from the wrong direction, the boat was powered by oars.

Wooden Ships. The boats of the ancient Egyptians had crude wooden hulls. The Phoenicians were the first to build hulls of heavy

The two types of vessels in this photo, ferry boats and cruise ships, are designed to carry passengers rather than cargo.

galley *ship with oars and sails, used in ancient and medieval times*

maneuverable *able to make a series of changes in course easily*

lateen-rigged *having triangular sails that can catch wind from either side of a mast, making a ship easy to maneuver*

square-rigged *having rectangular sails*

wooden planks covering an internal wooden framework. This plank-on-frame system remained the basic method of constructing ships for a few thousand years.

From the time of the Phoenicians to about the mid-1800s A.D., all seafaring ships were made of wood. The **galley** of the Phoenicians and Greeks served as the standard warship design for centuries. Powered by two or three banks of oars on each side, these long, narrow ships—called biremes and triremes—had a square sail for traveling when the wind was favorable. But during battle these vessels always used their oars—both for speed and for **maneuverability.** Phoenician and Greek ships were sturdy but not especially large. By strengthening the internal framework of the hull, the Romans managed to extend the limits of wooden ships, building cargo vessels and warships more than 200 feet (61 m) long.

By about A.D. 1000, sails had largely replaced oars as the main methods of moving ships. The cog, a type of sailing ship developed in the 1200s, was a sturdy northern European merchant vessel with raised platforms called castles on the deck. At about the same time, ships in the Mediterranean region began to feature triangular sails called lateens.

By the 1400s shipbuilders had combined features of the cog and **lateen-rigged** vessels and developed the three-masted, **square-rigged** sailing ship. This remained a standard ship design for the next 400 years. With the addition of rows of cannons, the design was also used for warships from the 1600s to the mid-1800s.

Ships of Iron and Steel. By the mid-1800s the largest ships—huge warships more than 300 feet (91 m) long—had reached the practical limits of wood construction. Small ships with iron hulls had been built in the early 1800s, and for a time, iron framing was also used in wooden ships. But it was the success of the iron ship *Great Britain,* launched in 1843, that really started the trend toward all-metal ships.

At the time the steam-powered *Great Britain*, equipped with a screw propeller, was the largest ship afloat—322 feet (98 m) long. Screw propellers had many advantages over the paddle wheels used on steamboats up to that time, including the ability to deliver more power and speed with the same size engine. Like most early oceangoing steamships, the *Great Britain* also carried sails in case of mechanical breakdowns on long sea voyages.

The development of steam-powered ships marked the beginning of the end for the great sailing vessels. As steam engines became more powerful and efficient, steamships began to compete for shipping traffic. By the late 1800s, thousands of voyages under steam power had demonstrated the reliability of this form of **propulsion.**

propulsion process of driving or propelling

Steel, which was stronger than iron, started to replace iron in ship construction in the late 1800s. The great strength of steel meant that less of it was needed, making ships lighter and less expensive to operate. The British liner *Servia*, built entirely of steel, made its first **transatlantic** voyage in 1881.

transatlantic relating to crossing the Atlantic Ocean

The age of sail was coming to an end. By 1887 the total cargo tonnage carried by steamships surpassed that of sailing ships for the first time. The amount of cargo carried by sailing ships worldwide declined steadily from 1892 onward, while that of steam- and motor-powered ships grew dramatically.

Modern Ships and Boats. Modern ships and boats range from huge supertankers, aircraft carriers, and cruise ships to small pleasure boats. Large commercial and naval vessels are constructed mainly of steel and other metals, and almost all have fuel-powered engines. Pleasure boats, however, are built of various materials, including wood, and they may be powered by oars, paddles, sails, or engines.

One of the most striking changes in ships and boats has been the increase in small pleasure craft. Until the mid-1900s, motorboats, sailboats, and large yachts belonged primarily to the wealthy. Since that time, however, improved production techniques and the introduction of strong, less expensive materials—such as plywood and fiberglass—have made boats more affordable and helped turn boating into a popular recreation and sport.

Powering Ships and Boats

During the 1800s steam engines evolved from a novelty to the main means of propelling most ships and boats. The first steam-powered ships appeared in the early 1800s. It was not until mid-century, however, that they began to dominate the waterways of the world and brought the great age of sail to an end.

Steam-Powered Ships. Steamships offered something that sailing ships could not—a relatively quick journey regardless of wind conditions. Sail-powered **packet** ships began making regular transatlantic trips in the 1830s, but the voyage from England to New York usually

packet small, fast ship used during the 1800s to carry mail, cargo, and passengers

took from four to six weeks. Within a decade the first oceangoing passenger steamships were making the same crossing in just 15 to 18 days. Steamships soon captured most of the transatlantic passenger business, though the packet ships continued to transport passengers until the 1860s.

The early steamships still used sails part of the time during long ocean voyages because they could not carry enough coal to fuel their engines for the entire trip. Moreover, early steam engines were not especially efficient, and their relative lack of power limited both the speed and the size of ships. Ocean-going vessels continued to carry masts and rigging for sails until the 1880s.

During the 1860s and 1870s, compound steam engines were introduced. These engines could produce much more power than earlier engines, allowing ships to go faster. Moreover, the use of coal was cut in half, increasing the traveling range and cargo capacity of ships driven by these engines.

Compound steam engines were followed by the steam turbine engine, developed by British engineer Charles Parsons in the late 1890s. The steam turbine used much less fuel and delivered significantly more power than a conventional steam engine, and it was also much simpler mechanically. These steam turbines could achieve previously unheard-of speeds—for example, the luxury ocean liner *Mauretania*, launched in 1907, could travel at a top speed of 27 **knots**. Gas turbines, which use hot gases instead of steam, were developed for use in ships later.

Naval officers have responsibilities ranging from navigation and communications to ship repairs and maintenance.

knot *unit of measure of a ship's speed, equal to about 1.15 miles (1.85 km) per hour*

maritime *related to the sea or shipping*

Other Forms of Propulsion.

Another important change in ship propulsion came about in the early 1900s, when the diesel engine was adapted for **maritime** use. Large diesel engines took up less space than turbine engines and consumed less fuel as well. In addition, fewer crew members were needed to run diesel engines because the heavy oil that they burned as fuel simply flowed through pipes to the engine—it did not have to be shoveled by hand like the coal in steam-powered ships.

The first ships outfitted with marine diesel engines went into operation in 1910, and diesel soon became the preferred type of engine for merchant ships. One of the earliest diesel-powered ships, the *Selandia* of Denmark, made a 26,000-mile (41,830-km) voyage from Europe to Asia in 1912 without stopping to refuel. Today, many of the world's cargo ships run on diesel engines, and diesels also power ocean liners, ferries, tugboats, commercial fishing boats, and a large number of motorized yachts.

Many large naval ships use gas turbines, which take up little space and generate very high speeds. Some naval vessels have steam turbine engines powered by small nuclear reactors. Until the arrival of nuclear power, ships had a limited cruising range because of the need to refuel. Nuclear-powered ships, however, can operate for years at a time on only a small amount of nuclear fuel. Except for repairs, replenishing food and supplies, and rotating crew members, nuclear-powered submarines, aircraft carriers, and other naval vessels do not have to return to port. Their reactors and steam turbines can keep a ship under way almost indefinitely.

The Ship's Crew

All large ships are operated by a crew consisting of officers of different ranks and seamen who perform the various day-to-day tasks aboard ship. The crews on sailing ships in the past often had to endure miserable conditions—bad food, cramped living quarters, low pay, and long hours. The living and working conditions and pay have improved considerably for crews in modern times.

The commanding officer of a ship—the ship's master or captain—has full authority over the ship and its crew, as well as any cargo or passengers. Several officers, called mates, assist the captain. The first mate is second in command and has charge of all parts of the ship except the engine room. The second mate serves as navigator and is responsible for charting the ship's course and position. Additional mates have other duties. Each takes a turn standing watch, which means being in charge of the ship while the captain and other mates are asleep or otherwise occupied.

Crews are divided into various departments. The deck department has responsibility for navigation and for maintaining and repairing the ship. Its crew consists of deckhands, or seamen, who perform various tasks to keep the ship operating; a boatswain, who acts as foreman of the deckhands; a ship's carpenter; and a quartermaster, who steers the ship. The engine department, run by a chief engineer and assistants, has charge of the operation and maintenance of the ship's engines and other machinery. The radio department handles the ship's communications, and the steward's department is responsible for cooking and housekeeping. Large passenger ships also have a purser's department, which takes care of bookkeeping and other paperwork, and a medical department.

The crew of an average cargo ship ranges in size from about 35 to 55 members—much smaller than during the age of great sailing ships. As automation increases, the size of cargo ship crews continues to decrease. Big cruise ships, however, have very large crews to attend to thousands of passengers.

Ship Communications

In centuries past, once a ship sailed away from port, communication with the world was cut off almost completely. The only way a ship at sea could communicate with land was to hail a passing ship and send messages back to a port. Even communication between ships at sea could be difficult. In rough weather, it was often too dangerous to bring sailing ships close enough to communicate by voice. At night or in foggy

Why Do Ships Float?

Drop a steel bar in water and it sinks like a rock. Yet a steel ship weighing thousands of tons floats. Why? Because of a phenomenon called buoyancy. A piece of wood floats in water because it displaces—pushes aside—a volume of water that weighs as much as it does. That gives the wood the buoyancy needed to float.

If a ship were one solid piece of steel, it would sink too. But it is really a hollow steel container that displaces a huge amount of water—so much that even when loaded with cargo, the weight of the ship and all it holds is still less than the weight of the displaced water. For this reason, the force of buoyancy makes the ship float.

weather, seeing another ship—much less communicating with it—was almost impossible.

Sailors devised a number of ways to communicate with flags and lights. In the 1600s ships began to use flag signals to send brief messages during the daytime, when visibility permitted. Eventually two signaling systems developed—one based on flags of certain colors and designs; and one, known as semaphore, in which flags are held in different positions that correspond to words or letters of the alphabet.

Communicating between ships at night posed another problem. For centuries mariners sent signals by arranging lanterns in patterns. By the 1860s they developed a standardized system of light signals, consisting of long or short flashes of light in differing order. Signalmen aboard ships opened and closed the shutters of special lanterns to spell out messages, which could be seen over long distances at night. With the introduction of powerful electric searchlights, light signals could be used even in the daytime.

The invention of radio revolutionized ship communications, making it possible to send messages almost anywhere—even when a ship was far out at sea—and in all kinds of weather. The first shipboard radios used the dots and dashes of Morse code to spell out messages. With the development of voice radio in the early 1900s, it became possible for ships to communicate without resorting to such codes.

Ships still rely mainly on radio for communications, but the power and range of modern radio systems are much greater than in the past. Moreover, special radio frequencies are set aside just for maritime communications, and commercial and noncommercial vessels have separate channels. Ships sometimes still use flag and light signals, as well as bells, whistles, and foghorns, to send messages.

Radio signals also play a role in navigation. Special radio signals are transmitted continuously from stations along seacoasts, helping ships determine their positions. One such system, known as loran (long range navigation), allows ships to pinpoint their locations in all types of weather. Radio signals transmitted from orbiting satellites are also helpful in guiding ships. *See also* AIRCRAFT CARRIERS; BARGES; CANOES AND KAYAKS; CARGO SHIPS; CATAMARANS; CLIPPER SHIPS; COMMUNICATION SYSTEMS; CRUISE SHIPS; ENGINES; FERRIES; FISHING BOATS; GREAT EASTERN; HARBORS AND PORTS; HYDROFOILS; LORAN; MARITIME HAZARDS; MERCHANT MARINE; MOTORBOATS; NAVIES; NAVIGATION; OCEAN LINERS; RAFTS; SAILBOATS AND SAILING SHIPS; SHIPBUILDING; SHIPPING INDUSTRY; SHIPS AND BOATS, PARTS OF; SHIPS AND BOATS, SAFETY OF; SHIPS AND BOATS, TYPES OF; SIGNALING; SUBMARINES AND SUBMERSIBLES; TANKERS; TUGBOATS; YACHTS.

Ships and Boats, Parts of

propulsion process of driving or propelling

Away at sea for days or even weeks, large ships must be able to function on their own. They need to carry basic provisions, such as food for the crew and passengers and fuel for the engines. They must also have equipment to generate electricity, supply heat or air-conditioning inside the ship, dispose of garbage, and sometimes make freshwater from seawater. Because of these needs, large ships are among the most complicated forms of transportation. They bear little outward resemblance to small boats. Yet most types of ships and boats have certain basic parts—a hull, a deck, a **propulsion** system, and steering equipment.

Parts of an Ocean Liner

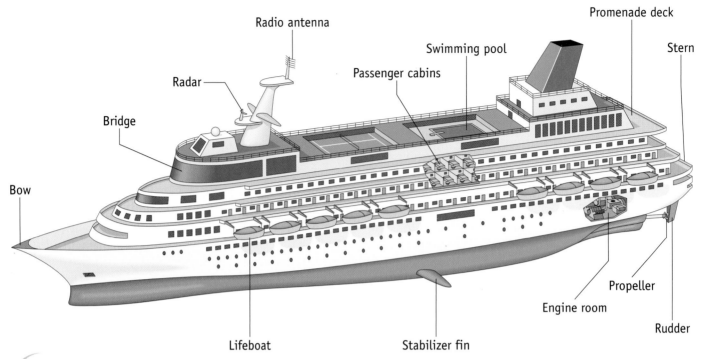

Ocean liners have all of the comforts of a resort hotel, including deluxe passenger cabins, dining rooms, theaters, fitness clubs, and swimming pools.

The Hull. The most important part of any ship is its body, or hull—a watertight shell that helps to keep the vessel afloat. The hulls of ships house cargo, machinery, fuel, and sometimes living spaces for passengers and crew. Before the 1800s the hulls of all ships were made of wood. Today most large ships have hulls of steel; the hulls of smaller boats may be metal, wood, fiberglass, or ferroconcrete—a type of reinforced concrete.

The hulls of ships and boats usually have a bow, a pointed front that enables the vessel to cut through the water easily. The stern, or rear, of most hulls is rounded, which allows water to close behind the vessel more smoothly as it travels through the water.

Strength and stability are among the most important characteristics of a ship's hull. Interior vertical walls, called bulkheads, run crosswise inside the hull, adding to its strength. These walls help support the sides of the hull and divide the interior space into compartments. On large ships the compartments are designed so that they can be sealed off by watertight doors if the hull is damaged and water begins to flood the ship. This important safety measure helps a ship stay afloat when some compartments become flooded. However, if the damage is severe and too many compartments fill with water, the ship will sink.

To further increase the strength of the structure, many ships have a double hull—two layers of steel or wood with an air space between them. This adds an extra measure of safety, making it more unlikely that damage to the hull will endanger the ship. Fuel and water are often stored in the spaces between the two layers of such hulls.

Various elements of a ship can affect its stability. Stability refers to the ability of a ship to float upright and to withstand the stresses caused by wind and waves without rolling from side to side. The shape of the hull can help reduce a ship's tendency to roll. In addition, extra weight—called ballast—is added to ships to make them ride lower in the water and roll less in rough seas. This is often done by pumping seawater into tanks inside the ship's hull. The cargo on fully loaded ships acts as ballast.

Bilge keels and stabilizers also play a part in keeping ships from rolling too much. Bilge keels are fins mounted on the underside of the hull at the point where it begins to curve upward. Stabilizers are fins mounted on the sides of the hull just below the waterline. Stabilizer fins are often controlled electronically. When a ship starts to roll and one side dips downward, the stabilizer on that side automatically tilts upward, while the other tilts downward. The movement of the stabilizer fins helps stop the roll or at least minimizes it.

Decks and Superstructure.

The space inside the hull contains horizontal floor surfaces called decks as well as vertical bulkheads. On many large ships, the decks are equipped with hatches—watertight doors that can be closed if a compartment floods. The uppermost deck, the one at the top of the hull and level with its sides, is known as the main deck.

A ship's superstructure includes all structures above the main deck that extend the full width of the ship. Other structures on the main deck are called deckhouses. The superstructures and deckhouses of modern ships developed from raised platforms at the bow (forecastle) and stern (sterncastle) of sailing ships in earlier centuries.

Located high up in the ship's superstructure is the bridge, which houses navigational equipment and the controls for steering the ships and changing engine speed. From the bridge the captain and other officers have a clear view of the waters ahead. Sometimes navigational and communications equipment is found in other rooms within the superstructure. The forecastle and the poop—a partly or completely enclosed space at the stern of the ship—contain living quarters for the crew and storage areas for equipment and supplies.

On ocean liners and cruise ships, the ship's superstructure includes passenger compartments. Also located on the superstructure or the main deck are smokestacks, funnels for drawing in air to ventilate compartments, radio and radar antennae, lifeboats, anchors, and various other equipment.

Propulsion.

The ship's propulsion system provides the push that moves the vessel through the water. At one time oars, poles, and sails were the only means of propelling ships and boats. Today a wide range of other systems is also available. Depending on the size and type of vessel, power might be provided by a gasoline engine, diesel engine, steam turbine, gas turbine, or nuclear reactor.

Small pleasure boats generally rely on oars or paddles, sails, or gasoline engines for propulsion. Larger motor yachts, tugboats, commercial fishing boats, and small- to medium-sized ships are usually powered by diesel engines. Large passenger liners and warships have steam or gas turbine engines or, in the case of some warships, nuclear propulsion systems.

Related Entries
For information on related topics, refer to the articles mentioned at the end of this entry.

In ships with steam turbines, fuel is burned to heat water in a boiler deep in the ship's hull. The steam produced by this action is used to spin one or more turbines—machines with rotating blades—in the ship's engine room. Gas turbines are turned by hot gases rather than steam. In nuclear-powered ships, the nuclear reactor provides the heat needed to create steam for the turbines.

The shaft of each turbine is connected to a gearbox, which controls the number of revolutions per minute. A long metal shaft runs from the gearbox through the bottom of the ship's stern to the propeller—a device with rotating blades. Each propeller is connected to a separate shaft. Large ships usually have two or four propellers; small ships and boats often have only one.

Some ships are equipped with turboelectric systems, which consist of turbines that power an electric generator. Electric motors use the electricity produced to turn the propeller shaft. Other ships are equipped with diesel-electric systems, which have a diesel engine that operates the generator and produces electricity to turn the propellers.

As a ship's propeller blades spin, they drive the ship forward by a screwlike action. The blades literally slice forward through the water, pushing the ship ahead of them. Rotating the propeller blades in the opposite direction makes the ship move backward.

On most ships the propellers are open to the water on all sides. But on tugboats and low-speed vessels that require extra pushing power, the propellers may be mounted inside tubes under the stern. This arrangement greatly increases the amount of power produced by the engine at slow speeds. At higher cruising speeds, however, propeller tubes do not have the same advantage. Some high-speed racing boats possess jet engines instead of conventional propeller systems.

Steering Equipment. The most important part of the ship's steering gear is the rudder—a long vertical fin mounted in the stern of the vessel. The rudder is controlled by the steering gear and the ship's helm, or wheel. Turning the helm to the right or left while a ship is moving will turn the rudder in the same direction, causing the ship to go in that direction as well. Small boats and ships react quickly to movements of the rudder. Large ships take much longer to respond to changes in direction.

Ships with two propellers can use them for turning the vessel quickly or **maneuvering** at slow speeds alongside a dock or in other tight places. Putting the left propeller in reverse and the right propeller in forward will turn the bow to the left. Some large ocean liners have devices called bow thrusters, small propellers mounted in tubes running crosswise near the bow of the ship. The thrusters help in docking and other tight maneuvers.

Other Parts and Equipment. All boats and ships carry lifeboats or other safety equipment, such as pumps for pumping up seawater to fight fires. Most ships and boats have radio equipment for communicating with land and other vessels and navigational equipment for determining location. Ships and boats may also contain electrical equipment to supply heat, air-conditioning, light, refrigeration, and other

Nuclear-Powered Cargo Ships

The world's first nuclear-powered cargo ship, the USS *Savannah,* was built by the U.S. government to demonstrate possible peacetime uses of nuclear power. Just under 600 feet (183 m) long, the ship could carry 9,400 tons of cargo and up to 60 passengers. Launched in 1959, the *Savannah* made a number of demonstration cruises during the 1960s. But its operating costs proved to be much greater than those of cargo ships powered by conventional engines, and the ship was taken out of service. Although Russia, Germany, and Japan have also built nuclear-powered cargo ships, these have turned out to be impractical because of their high cost.

maneuver to make a series of changes in course

winch machine for lifting or pulling

shipboard necessities. Various kinds of mechanical devices—including **winches,** pulleys, and rollers—may be on deck for securing ropes and chains, raising and lowering anchors, and performing other tasks.

Depending on the type of ship or boat, vessels may be fitted with a wide range of other parts and equipment. Cargo ships often possess large cranes for loading and unloading freight. Battleships may be armed with missile launchers and other weapons. Cruise ships usually include swimming pools and recreational equipment. Sailing ships have masts, sails, and numerous ropes for controlling the sails. *See also* BALLAST; CARGO SHIPS; COMMUNICATION SYSTEMS; CRUISE SHIPS; ENGINES; FISHING BOATS; LORAN; MOTORBOATS; NAVIGATION; SAILBOATS AND SAILING SHIPS; SHIPS AND BOATS, TYPES OF; STEAMBOATS; TANKERS.

Ships and Boats, Safety of

maritime related to the sea or shipping

territorial waters inland and coastal waters under the authority of a state or nation

Traveling on water, whether in a small boat or a large ship, involves certain risks. Bad weather, collisions, or fire can cause injuries to passengers and damage or sink a vessel.

To prevent accidents and protect passengers and crew, ships and boats must meet a wide range of safety standards. Many of these standards are set by worldwide **maritime** organizations, such as the International Convention for the Safety of Life at Sea. The laws and regulations of individual countries often spell out additional safety requirements. In the United States, the federal government and the Coast Guard set regulations relating to ship safety. The Coast Guard also enforces rules concerning the construction and operation of vessels within U.S. **territorial waters.**

Safety Rules and Equipment. Ships are required by various national and international regulations to carry safety equipment and to follow procedures designed to prevent accidents. Fire is a major

Ships and boats are required to carry a life jacket for every person on board. During practice drills, passengers learn how to use the jackets and other safety equipment.

maritime hazard. Ships must contain fire detection systems, firefighting equipment, and automatic extinguishing systems such as sprinklers. As a further precaution, ships are built with as many fire retardant materials as possible.

Preventing collisions between ships is another important concern. Captains must follow a set of international "rules of the road." Ships approaching head on are required to pass each other with their port (left) sides together. Ships must use their running lights at night—a red light on the port side and a green one on the starboard (right) side—and sound a foghorn or siren when moving through fog. Sound signals are also used to warn nearby ships of a change in course.

Various procedures and equipment help prevent ships from running aground. Marine charts clearly mark all known hazards, such as rocks, reefs, and shallow areas, and navigational aids such as the Global Positioning System (GPS) help ships avoid dangerous areas and stay on course. Radar can warn of large rocks, landmasses, and approaching ships even at night or in foggy weather. In addition, lighthouses, **buoys,** and radio beacons all warn ships of hazards.

buoy floating marker in the water

Overloading a ship with cargo or passengers can make it ride too low in the water and cause it to capsize in rough weather. For this reason, international rules have established load limits for vessels. Each ship has lines on the side of its hull that indicate how deep the ship can ride safely in different seasons and waters. Called Plimsoll marks, the lines are named for Samuel Plimsoll, a British politician who supported safer conditions at sea. Ships can ride deeper in summer, when storms are less severe, than they can in winter.

To prevent vessels from sinking, shipbuilders construct the hulls with watertight compartments. If part of the hull is torn open, water will not flow into the rest of the ship. Oil tankers have double hulls to prevent the release of oil into the sea in case of an accident.

Oil tankers have built-in safety features—such as double hulls—to minimize the amount of oil released during an accident. If an oil spill occurs, many people are called in to help with the cleanup.

Emergency Procedures. Sometimes vessels are so badly damaged during an accident that the passengers and crew must abandon ship. Standard marine distress signals are used to call for help from other ships in the area. All ships and boats are required to carry a life-jacket for every person aboard. Ships must also have lifeboats and other lifesaving equipment for the maximum number of passengers and crew members. When the Coast Guard is on the scene, it may launch additional rescue boats to assist people aboard disabled ships and boats. *See also* ACCIDENTS; COAST GUARD; COMMUNICATION SYSTEMS; CONVOYS; EMERGENCY TRANSPORTATION; GLOBAL POSITIONING SYSTEM (GPS); LIGHTHOUSES AND LIGHTSHIPS; MAPS AND CHARTS; MARITIME HAZARDS; MARITIME LAW; REGULATION OF TRANSPORTATION; SHIPS AND BOATS; SHIPWRECKS; SIGNALING.

Ships and Boats, Types of

propulsion process of driving or propelling

There are hundreds of different types of ships and boats, from small rowboats and sailboats to huge cruise ships, aircraft carriers, and supertankers. These vessels can be classified in a number of ways, such as by size or by the kind of **propulsion** used. They also can be grouped by function. Most ships and boats fall into four broad categories of function: commercial cargo ships, commercial passenger ships, military vessels, and pleasure craft.

Commercial Cargo Ships. A variety of ships carry goods across the world's oceans, seas, and inland waterways. These vessels are usually classified according to the type of cargo they transport.

General cargo ships are vessels that haul a mixture of goods, such as automobiles, electronic equipment, sacks of coffee, cases of wine, and other agricultural products or manufactured items. Loading and unloading this varied cargo involves considerable time and labor and, consequently, high costs. Once the most important type of freighter, general cargo ships have declined in numbers in recent decades. Many have been replaced by specialized ships that carry only a particular type of product.

Tankers were among the first ships designed to transport a single type of cargo. These vessels haul liquid products, primarily oil. Supertankers are among the largest ships in the world. Some measure as much as 1,500 feet (457 m) in length and can carry more than 500,000 tons of liquid. The use of tankers and supertankers has made the shipment of oil and other liquids cheaper and more efficient. But the ships have certain disadvantages. The largest supertankers can only enter deepwater ports, and the risk of a major oil spill in the event of an accident makes them a potential threat to the environment.

Dry bulk carriers haul iron ore, fertilizers, grain, and other kinds of loose, bulky material. First developed in the late 1800s for carrying iron ore on the Great Lakes, the vessels now transport cargoes all over the world. The largest oceangoing dry bulk carriers can hold as much as 100,000 tons of material. A special dry bulk carrier known as the O/B/O is designed to carry both bulk cargo, such as grain or ore, and oil.

Container ships carry goods packed in large metal boxes called containers. Cranes stack the containers in open compartments in the hull of the ship and on its main deck. Because goods are packed into the containers before they reach the ship, the time and labor involved in

facilities something built or created to serve a particular function

handling the cargo is dramatically reduced. Cranes can load as many as 1,000 containers onto a ship in a matter of hours. The quick loading and unloading allows the vessels to make faster round-trips between ports, reducing shipping costs.

Roll-on/roll-off ships are a modified type of container ship. Their hulls have openings with ramps that make it possible to drive vehicles or wheeled containers—such as truck trailers—directly on board the ship, eliminating the need for special cranes and other expensive port **facilities.** The largest roll-on/roll-off ships can hold about 1,000 cars and trucks or 1,100 large wheeled containers.

Another specialized cargo ship is the LASH, which stands for lighter aboard ship. These vessels transport lighters, or barges, filled with almost any type of cargo. The lighters are hoisted on board by cranes. When the ship reaches port, the lighters are unloaded and then towed to their final destination by tugboats or other vessels. LASH ships, which hold from 70 to 90 lighters, can be loaded very quickly and efficiently.

Commercial Passenger Ships. There are two main types of commercial passenger ships: liners and ferries. From the early 1900s to the 1950s, large and luxurious passenger ships called ocean liners made regularly scheduled trips between various world ports. By the 1970s most of these great ships had been retired, overcome by airline competition. Since then, however, a new generation of luxury passenger liners called cruise ships have appeared. Basically floating hotels, cruise ships offer tours to the Caribbean, the Mediterranean, and other popular spots. Unlike the ocean liners of the past, cruise ships provide vacation travel and entertainment rather than transportation. The largest vessels can accommodate as many as 2,000 passengers.

Ferries are ships and boats of various sizes that carry passengers, and sometimes cars or other vehicles, on established routes across harbors, lakes, rivers, and small seas. Car ferries have openings with ramps in the side, front, or back that allow passengers to drive their vehicles directly on board. The largest car ferries can hold as many as 350 cars and 800 passengers. Ferries that make long, overnight voyages often have cabins for passengers. Large ferries may include several passenger decks with dining areas, lounges, and other facilities.

In some places hydrofoils or air-cushion vehicles provide ferry service. Hydrofoils are high-speed vessels that skim above the surface of the water on wing-shaped structures attached to the hull. The ships can reach speeds exceeding 80 **knots.** Air-cushion vehicles (ACVs), also called hovercraft, travel over the water on a cushion of air produced by powerful fans beneath the vessel. Because they ride on a cushion of air, ACVs can operate over very shallow water and even travel over land.

knot unit of measure of a ship's speed, equal to about 1.15 miles (1.85 km) per hour

Military Vessels. The world's navies contain many types of ships, from patrol boats to submarines. Each is specially designed and outfitted for a particular function. The best known military vessels are battleships, aircraft carriers, cruisers, destroyers, and submarines.

The first modern battleship, the British *Dreadnought,* was launched in 1906. In the decades that followed, navies built many large, heavily armored ships equipped with large guns and other heavy firearms. Yet

Speedboats are small pleasure craft often used for racing. This speedboat is competing in a timed event on the Potomac River.

the ships did not dominate naval warfare for long. Aircraft carriers were introduced in 1941, and battleships could not withstand attacks by planes launched from the carriers. After World War II, most battleships were retired from active service.

Aircraft carriers are huge floating airfields. Their flat upper deck, called the flight deck, serves as a takeoff and landing strip for jet fighter planes. The largest warships afloat, aircraft carriers may measure up to 1,000 feet (300 m) long and can transport some 100 fighter planes and several thousand sailors.

Fast warships with moderately heavy firearms are known as cruisers. They have taken the place of battleships as the largest conventionally armed warships. Many cruisers are also outfitted with guided missiles. These ships usually provide both antiaircraft defense and gunfire support for aircraft carriers. Light cruisers are faster, less heavily armed cruisers that are used frequently for scouting missions.

Destroyers are relatively small, fast warships designed mainly for defensive purposes. They usually carry antiaircraft and antisubmarine weaponry as well as guided missiles. Destroyers often defend aircraft carrier fleets and serve as escort ships for unarmed merchant vessels and naval supply ships.

Submarines are specialized vessels capable of operating underwater for extended periods. They played an important role in both world wars. With the development of nuclear-powered submarines in the 1950s, the range and effectiveness of the vessels increased greatly. Their ability to launch nuclear warheads on guided missiles has made submarines a key naval weapon.

Pleasure Craft.

Millions of boating enthusiasts around the world own pleasure boats that they use for recreation and sport. The three main types of pleasure craft are boats propelled by paddles or oars, motorboats, and sailboats.

The simplest and least expensive pleasure boats are rowboats, canoes, and kayaks. Rowboats, small vessels powered by oars, may be 7 to 16 feet (2 to 5 m) long. Most are designed for general purposes, such as fishing or rowing to a favorite spot on a lake. Canoes and kayaks are propelled by paddles instead of oars.

The majority of pleasure boats in the United States are motorboats. These range in size from 14-foot (4-m) runabouts with outboard motors to large cabin cruisers and motor yachts more than 100 feet (30 m) long. People generally use runabouts and other small motorboats for fishing, waterskiing, and other recreational activities. Larger cabin cruisers and motor yachts have comfortable living quarters and can undertake long voyages.

Sailboats are classified according to how they are rigged—that is, the number of masts and sails they have and how the sails are arranged. The smallest boats, called catboats, have one mast and one sail. They are very popular with beginning sailors because they are small and easy to handle. Other classes of sailboats include sloops, ketches, yawls, and schooners.

Other Types of Ships and Boats.

There are many other types of ships and boats, some of which serve very specific purposes. Tugboats haul barges and guide large ships entering ports. Icebreakers are ships with specially built hulls that can cut through ice-choked waterways. Fishing trawlers have special rigging that releases and pulls in nets for catching fish. Fish factory ships are designed to clean, cut, and package fish at sea. Other specialized ships and boats include research vessels engaged in **oceanography;** lightships that aid navigation at sea; salvage ships that retrieve the cargo of damaged or sunken ships; and fireboats, police boats, and rescue craft. *See also* AIRCRAFT CARRIERS; AIR-CUSHION VEHICLES; BARGES; CANOES AND KAYAKS; CARGO SHIPS; CATAMARANS; CLIPPER SHIPS; CONTAINERIZATION; CRUISE SHIPS; FERRIES; FISHING BOATS; FLATBOATS; FRIGATES; HYDROFOILS; ICEBREAKERS; LIGHTHOUSES AND LIGHTSHIPS; MERCHANT MARINE; MOTORBOATS; NAVIES; OCEAN LINERS; PASSENGERS; ROWBOATS; SAILBOATS AND SAILING SHIPS; SCHOONERS; SHIPPING INDUSTRY; SHIPS AND BOATS; SHIPS AND BOATS, PARTS OF; SHOWBOATS; STEAMBOATS; SUBMARINES AND SUBMERSIBLES; TANKERS; TUGBOATS; YACHTS.

What Does it Weigh?

There are several ways to measure the weight of a cargo or passenger ship. One is deadweight tonnage—the total weight of the cargo, fuel, supplies, equipment, crew, and passengers. This is the ship's carrying capacity, or the maximum amount it can safely carry. Another measure, displacement tonnage, refers to the weight of water that an unloaded ship will displace as it floats. This figure equals the weight of the ship itself.

Gross tonnage is the volume of all the ship's enclosed spaces; net tonnage is the gross tonnage minus the volume of all areas that do not contain cargo or passengers. The net tonnage measures the actual revenue-producing space on a ship, and it is used as the basis for various fees and taxes the ship must pay.

oceanography *scientific study of the ocean and underwater life*

Shipwrecks

maritime *related to the sea or shipping*

A shipwreck is the destruction or loss of a ship by some cause other than war. The history of **maritime** travel is dotted with tales of shipwreck, just as the ocean floor is littered with the remains of the sunken vessels. Despite advances in shipbuilding and maritime practices over the centuries, shipwreck remains a threat to modern watercraft. However, improved weather forecasting, navigation, communications, and

Shipwrecks may be caused by collisions between vessels, fires and explosions aboard ships, or rough seas and heavy fog. The wreck in this picture lies off the southwest coast of Ireland.

safety procedures have done much to reduce the chance of such a disaster.

Types and Causes of Shipwrecks.

In a total wreck the vessel is lost completely; in many cases it simply sinks. Some ships run aground and remain partly above water but are so badly damaged that they must be abandoned or destroyed to prevent them from posing a danger to other shipping. In a partial wreck, or partial loss, the vessel is damaged but may be recovered and repaired.

Shipwreck has many causes, and it is not always possible to determine the factors that led to a particular wreck. If passengers or crew members survive the disaster, their accounts may help investigators. Today some wrecks are preceded by radio broadcasts from the ships, describing the unfolding events. Physical evidence, such as floating wreckage or observation by divers of a sunken wreck, can also help to explain what happened. In many cases, however, ships simply vanish from the seas, often swiftly and without warning.

Maritime experts believe that the main cause of shipwrecks, both ancient and modern, is heavy seas—big, crashing waves stirred up by storms. Such conditions can produce freak or rogue waves, mountains of water more than 100 feet (30 m) high that can swamp even large ships. Fires and explosions aboard ships are another leading cause of shipwrecks, and countless vessels have been lost after running aground on a coastline or reef, perhaps in fog. Lighthouses and foghorns were invented in part to prevent such tragedies. Collisions between vessels have also caused many total and partial wrecks.

Famous Shipwrecks.   Perhaps the most famous shipwreck is that of the *Titanic,* a British passenger liner called "unsinkable" by its builders. During its first voyage in 1912, it sank within hours about 400 miles (640 km) south of Newfoundland after striking an iceberg in the North Atlantic Ocean. Some 1,500 people drowned. The sinking of the *Titanic* stunned the European and American public, in part because the ship's passenger list included a number of influential and wealthy men and women. But it was only one in a long series of dramatic disasters at sea.

Icebergs were the cause of other wrecks. In 1893 the *Naronic* disappeared while on the way from England to New York. Notes found floating in two bottles indicated that the ship had collided with an iceberg. The 55 crew members were never found. The *Naronic* belonged to the White Star company, which later built the equally ill-fated *Titanic.*

A notable shipwreck of more recent times was the collision in 1956 of the Italian passenger liner *Andrea Doria* and the Swedish liner *Stockholm* off the coast of Massachusetts. The 12,600-ton (11,428-metric ton) *Stockholm* struck the much larger Italian ship with its bow and tore its side. The next day a reporter circling the scene in a plane described the long process of evacuating the passengers from the sinking *Andrea Doria* and the ship's final descent under the waves. The age of broadcast and televised sea disasters had arrived.

Not all shipwrecks occur on the high seas. In 1904 a pleasure steamboat called the *General Slocum* burned in New York City's East River, with a death toll of 1,030. The ore carrier *Edmund Fitzgerald* and her crew of 29 went down during a storm on Lake Superior in 1975.

Many modern wrecks have involved ferry boats, vehicles that carry large numbers of passengers on short routes. In 1993, 253 people died when a ferry capsized off South Korea during a storm, and 97 perished when a ferry sank in the Philippines in 1998. Overcrowding may contribute to some ferry wrecks. Unfortunately, not all of these watercraft are fully equipped with safety gear such as life vests and lifeboats.

Finding Wrecks.   Since ancient times people have labored to retrieve valuable items from wrecked or sunken ships—at least in cases where the wreck's location was known and the vessel lay in fairly shallow water. By the second half of the 1900s, however, marine explorers and **salvagers** were using new technology to locate and recover ships once thought lost forever.

Treasure-hunting has always been a major motive for searching out wrecks, and a few salvagers have struck it rich with such prizes as gold-carrying Spanish **galleons** off the coast of Florida. In some cases, the study of wrecks has enormous historic and scientific value. Scholars have learned about the shipbuilding and trading practices of earlier eras by examining the remains of the *Vasa,* a Swedish warship that sank in

---

What Sank the Derbyshire?

On September 9, 1980, the British merchant ship *Derbyshire* disappeared in the Pacific Ocean south of Japan during a severe storm. All 44 people aboard lost their lives. A 1997 expedition to examine its wreck has provided clues to the cause of similar disasters. (Between 1980 and 1999, 180 cargo ships like the *Derbyshire* went down.) Photos taken by robot probes more than 13,000 feet (3,962 m) below the surface suggest that water entered the ship through openings in the bow, dragging the ship's nose down. Such studies may not only answer lingering questions about past wrecks but may help prevent future ones.

salvager *one who saves or recovers property lost underwater*

galleon *large sailing ship used for war and trade*

the Stockholm harbor in 1628, and a Bronze Age cargo ship that sank off the coast of Turkey about 3,000 years ago.

One of the most spectacular salvage feats of the late 1990s was the finding of the *Titanic.* Using small submarines called submersibles and remote-controlled robot cameras, researchers gave television and film audiences an eerie "tour" of the wreck and the debris that lies scattered around it on the ocean floor, including dinner plates and children's toys. Similar investigations of recent wrecks may provide information that will lead to safer shipbuilding and navigation. *See also* ACCIDENTS; FERRIES; LIGHT-HOUSES AND LIGHTSHIPS; MARITIME HAZARDS; SALVAGE; SHIPS AND BOATS, SAFETY OF; SUBMARINES AND SUB-MERSIBLES; TITANIC.

Showboats

tributary *stream or river that flows into a larger stream or river*

keelboat *narrow riverboat used to transport freight*

During the 1800s and early 1900s, showboats brought entertainment to river communities of the American Midwest and South. These floating theaters provided excitement, culture, and amusement. A showboat would tie up at a settlement along the Ohio River or the Mississippi River or one of their **tributaries,** put on performances, then move on to the next town.

The earliest showboat may have been a modified **keelboat** on which a group of performers traveled from Tennessee to Mississippi in the early 1800s. In 1831 William Chapman, Sr., a British actor, built the first boat designed specifically for entertainment. Called the *Floating Theatre,* it seated 200 people. Chapman's success led many others to launch their own showboats. One of the most spectacular was the *Floating Circus Palace,* which could seat 3,400 people and had a full-time staff of 100. Smaller showboats offered performances ranging from respectable plays and lectures to less wholesome entertainment accompanied by gambling and alcohol.

In the 1860s the Civil War temporarily halted showboating, but after the war a new wave of showboats took to the rivers. Operators used speedboats to drum up advance publicity and staged musical parades through towns to arouse interest. In 1910, 26 showboats were active on Midwestern rivers, but that number dropped to 14 in 1928 and to a mere 5 in 1938. Edna Ferber's 1926 novel *Showboat* drew on the colorful life of the river-borne entertainers. By the time the book appeared, however, the development of roads, automobiles, and movies was bringing an end to the era of the floating theater. A few vessels, such as the *Delta Queen,* still operate on the Mississippi and other rivers and have preserved some features of the old showboats.

Signaling

Signaling consists of a variety of visual, audible, and electrical devices that communicate information. Worldwide transportation systems rely on signaling to direct and control the movement of vehicles such as ships, trains, aircraft, and automobiles.

Early Methods and Development. Throughout history people have used various types of signals to send messages to one another.

The International Code of Signals, adopted in the late 1800s and still in use, represents letters and numbers with colored flags.

sonar short for sound navigation and ranging; system that uses sound waves to locate underwater objects

In ancient times, military commanders employed signals such as the sounding of trumpets and the use of smoke or banners to direct the movement of their troops.

By the mid-1500s nations had begun to adopt standard systems of signaling for communication between ships at sea. Flags were hung from masts, and the color, design, and arrangement of the flags indicated words or messages. The International Code of Signals, adopted in the late 1800s and still in use today, represents letters and numbers with flags and pennants.

Since the 1700s seafaring vessels have employed lights and sounds for signaling at night and in weather conditions that reduce the visibility of flags. Lights are arranged in patterns to transmit messages. The number and timing of foghorns, bells, whistles, or other sounds can communicate information as well.

Another visual system of signaling appeared in the late 1700s. Known as semaphore, it employed movable wooden arms on a post mounted on a tower. Messages were sent by changing the position of the arms. With the aid of telescopes, lookouts located at towers 5 to 10 miles (8 to 16 km) apart could receive and relay messages quickly. In the 1800s ships adopted a semaphore system in which a person holds a flag in each hand and moves them to different positions to indicate letters, numbers, and short phrases.

During the early days of railroading, engineers received instructions and information by means of colored flags. The flags were soon replaced by trackside signals consisting of bars or disks controlled by hand-operated levers.

Modern Signaling.   The introduction of the electric telegraph in 1844 marked the beginning of a new era in signaling. During the battles of World War I and World War II, telephones and radios enabled the military to coordinate troop movement on the ground, direct bombs from the air, and communicate across the seas. Radar and **sonar** also came into use during wartime. Aircraft, ships, and other vehicles use the signals sent out by radar to detect objects many miles away and determine their distance, direction, and speed. Sonar enabled seagoing vessels to locate submarines and explosive mines.

Automobiles and railroads have also benefited from electrical signals, most of which are controlled by computers. Traffic lights located at intersections on roads direct motor vehicle movement. Signals are usually set at timed intervals, which may be changed during rush hours. The mechanical signal systems used by railroads have given way to colored lights often regulated from a central traffic control center.

Since the 1960s the use of artificial satellites that orbit the Earth has dramatically affected signaling. With the ability to receive and transmit signals to and from ground stations over a wide area, communications satellites can relay information around the world. *See also* AIR TRAFFIC CONTROL; COMMUNICATION SYSTEMS; LORAN; NAVIGATION; RADAR; SATELLITES; SHIPS AND BOATS, SAFETY OF; SONAR.

Sikorsky, Igor Ivan
Russian aircraft designer

Russian engineer Igor Ivan Sikorsky developed the first successful helicopters and several important multiengine airplanes. Sikorsky's innovations in air transportation have been used by commercial airlines, the armed forces, and search and rescue operations.

Sikorsky was born in Kiev, Russia, in 1889. After learning of the achievements of the Wright brothers and other aviation pioneers in the early 1900s, Sikorsky tried to build a plane that could fly straight up—a helicopter. However, several attempts failed, and he admitted that he lacked the proper engines and materials, as well as money and experience.

In 1910 he turned his attention to airplane design, producing the first four-engine plane, *Le Grand,* three years later. During World War I Sikorsky built many bombers, but his work was halted by the Russian Revolution. Sikorsky immigrated to the United States in 1919, and after a short career as a teacher, he founded the Sikorsky Aero-Engineering Corporation. His new company flourished with the production of flying boats—airplanes that could take off and land on water. During the 1930s, Sikorsky's flying boats blazed **transoceanic** mail and passenger routes for Pan American World Airways.

By the late 1930s Sikorsky realized that military and commercial airlines were moving away from flying boats, so he returned to working on helicopters. Equipped with the proper materials and experience, he quickly produced the VS-300 helicopter in 1939. Sikorsky took great pride in this new form of air transportation and its heroic uses in rescue and relief missions. He did not anticipate the important role of helicopters in military combat, but he lived to see their dominance in the Vietnam War. Sikorsky died in 1972. *See also* AIRCRAFT, MILITARY; AIRCRAFT INDUSTRY; HELICOPTERS; SEAPLANES.

Igor Sikorsky, the Russian aircraft designer, is seen in this photo from the 1950s working on an airplane model.

transoceanic *extending across an ocean*

Silk Road

One of the most famous trade routes of the ancient world, the Silk Road served as a link between China and the West for more than 1,000 years. Beginning in the 100s B.C., merchants carried silks, porcelains, furs, and other items from Asia to Western markets, and wools, gold, and silver traveled eastward.

The Silk Road was not a road but a network of caravan routes that covered about 4,000 miles (6,436 km). Starting at Siking (now Xi'an), an ancient Chinese capital, the main trail continued northwest through the Takla Makan desert. From there it crossed the Pamirs mountains to modern Afghanistan. The Silk Road eventually reached the Mediterranean region, where it joined the trade routes of Europe, the Middle

East, and North Africa. Branches of the road fanned out in many directions to cities throughout central and southern Asia.

Travel over the Silk Road was difficult and dangerous. Merchants encountered harsh weather conditions, from scorching desert heat to bitter cold and snow in the mountains. They transported their goods at the risk of being robbed by the many bandits along the way. Because the trails were often little more than footpaths that disappeared suddenly, skilled guides were useful.

In early centuries most merchants used camels and other pack animals to transport their wares along the Silk Road. Later, goods were carried in carts pulled by oxen or horses. Few individuals traveled the entire route. Instead, goods passed through the hands of many different traders, each covering only a small portion of the journey.

Commerce over the Silk Road reached its height during the time of the Roman Empire. It remained an important trade route until Arab conquests in the Middle East made travel increasingly unsafe. Activity on the Silk Road was renewed in the 1200s, when Italian explorer Marco Polo traveled the route to China.

The Silk Road trade brought great prosperity to many cities in central Asia, including Bactra and Samarkand, as well as centers in Europe. In addition to encouraging the exchange of goods, the Silk Road became an avenue for the flow of ideas between Europe and Asia, making a significant impact on the civilizations of both regions.

In the 1400s Europeans discovered more direct sea routes to China. As a result, the Silk Road began to fade in importance, bringing economic decline to cities along its entire length. Russian conquests in central Asia during the 1800s finally brought all trade along the route to an end. *See also* CAMELS; CARAVANS; CRUSADES; TRADE AND COMMERCE; TRAVEL WRITING.

Skateboard

see Sports and Recreation.

Skates

see Sports and Recreation.

Skis

see Sports and Recreation.

Skylab

Skylab—the first and only U.S. space station—was launched on May 14, 1973. Although inhabited for less than six months during its six-year lifetime, *Skylab* provided valuable information about the long-term effects of spaceflight on astronauts.

The main body of *Skylab,* called the orbital workshop (OWS), was built from part of a Saturn V rocket. A tank that usually held liquid hydrogen became the living and work area. Equipment and waste were stored in an empty liquid oxygen tank. Measuring 118 feet (36 m) long and 22 feet (6.7 m) wide, the OWS could accommodate three astronauts. Its two solar panels provided electric power for the station. A multiple docking adapter (MDA) attached to the OWS enabled Apollo spacecraft to link up with *Skylab*. The space station also contained scientific equipment such as the Apollo Telescope Mount, an Apollo lunar module that had been adapted to hold telescopes for studying the Sun.

Skylab experienced problems immediately after launching. One of its solar panels ripped off during the launch, the other became jammed and would not open, and some insulation on the OWS was torn away. The first astronauts to visit *Skylab* repaired this damage in a number of long space walks. Their experience proved that humans could work effectively outside a spacecraft.

Three crews spent time aboard *Skylab* during its first nine months, making observations and measurements of the Earth and Sun and conducting experiments. Each group of astronauts set a new record for space endurance, with the final crew spending 84 days at the station. The United States hoped to keep *Skylab* in orbit long enough to send a space shuttle to dock with it. But the station fell from orbit in July 1979, two years before the launching of the first U.S. space shuttle. *See also* MIR; SALYUT SPACE STATIONS; SPACE EXPLORATION; SPACE STATIONS.

Slave Trade

Between the mid-1400s and the early 1800s, European and American ships transported Africans to the Americas to be sold as slaves. This thriving slave trade was related to the establishment of European colonies in the Americas. Plantations and mines in the colonies required large numbers of workers to produce crops and precious metals. In many places slaves helped fill this need.

Origins of the Slave Trade. In the 1400s Portuguese navigators became the first Europeans to explore the west coast of Africa and establish contact with African tribes. Some of the tribal rulers owned hundreds of slaves and began selling them to Portuguese traders. The Portuguese sold the slaves for good profit in Europe and established coastal outposts in western Africa, where they bartered for slaves.

After the Spanish settled in the Americas, they forced local Indians to work in their mines and farms. However, the enslaved Indians died in large numbers from diseases the Spanish brought from Europe. The colonists needed another source of labor.

In 1517 a Spanish priest named Bartolomé de Las Casas noticed that the African slaves in the colonies remained healthy while the Indians fell ill. Hoping to save the Indians, he suggested importing Africans to provide labor for the settlements. The following year King Charles I of Spain issued the first *asientos de negros,* royal contracts that gave the holder the right to bring slaves to the Spanish colonies.

From the 1520s onward, South America was the destination for most enslaved Africans. Portuguese traders dominated the early years of the **transatlantic** slave trade. The Dutch became involved in the mid-1600s, and Britain and France followed in the 1700s. Britain, a great sea power, soon took the lead in transporting enslaved Africans.

transatlantic relating to crossing the Atlantic Ocean

Slavery in North America.
At first, many of the immigrants to British North America were indentured servants—people who paid for their transatlantic passage by promising to work for a certain number of years. But during the 1700s, the rise of large plantations created a sudden need for more laborers. Colonists began to rely on slaves. By the late 1700s, about 60,000 enslaved Africans arrived on British, French, and American ships each year. During 300 years of active trading, the territories that became the United States received about 600,000 slaves, roughly 6 percent of those taken from Africa.

Slave ships also did business in the Caribbean. American traders operating out of Newport, Rhode Island, sailed there regularly. They began by exchanging beef and lumber from New England for molasses in the West Indies. They carried the molasses to Rhode Island, where it was converted into rum. Then they took the rum to Africa to trade for slaves, which were sold in the West Indies for more molasses. The three destinations formed a rough triangle, giving rise to the name *triangular trade.* Some traders focused on only one or two sections of the route. Boston merchants, and to a lesser degree those in New York, Philadelphia, and Charleston, also took part in slave trading.

Crossing the Atlantic.
In the slave trade, the voyage across the Atlantic Ocean from Africa to the Americas was known as the Middle Passage. At first traders used converted merchant ships, but later they began building ships especially designed for carrying slaves. Often these vessels were heavily armed, both to defend against raiders and to raid other slave ships for their human cargo.

The enslaved Africans endured horrible conditions during the lengthy voyage. They were tightly packed like sticks of wood in the ships' holds. Disease was widespread and those who refused to eat were force-fed. Often between 10 and 20 percent of the unwilling passengers died at sea.

End of the Slave Trade.
Opposition to slavery mounted in Britain, the United States, and elsewhere toward the end of the 1700s. But the economic importance of slaves made it difficult to bring an immediate end to slavery. The British began by attacking the source of supply—the slave trade, which they abolished in 1807. The United States ended the slave trade a year later, but slavery continued in some states until 1865. The transatlantic slave trade had all but disappeared by that time, as other countries joined the ban. However, the smuggling of slaves continued for years. *See also* ATLANTIC OCEAN; CARGO SHIPS.

Sleighs

Sleighs, also called sleds or sledges, are vehicles that travel across a surface, such as snow or ice, on long, narrow runners. When pulled by teams of dogs, horses, or reindeer, sleighs can carry heavy loads of cargo as well as passengers. Once a primary means of transportation, most of these vehicles are now used for recreation or sport.

Origin and Development.
Sleighs probably developed from the travois, a simple device consisting of two long poles harnessed at

Held every March, the Iditarod Trail Dog Sled Race features a 1,100-mile (1,770-km) course that goes from Anchorage to Nome, Alaska.

one end to a horse or other animal. Items to be transported are attached to the other end of the poles. Early Native Americans used the travois and the toboggan—a flat-bottomed sled without runners—to carry game and supplies.

The ancient peoples of northern Europe, Egypt, and the Middle East employed a type of sledge to haul very heavy loads across snow, ice, grass, sand, and swamps. The Egyptians, for example, built massive vehicles with sturdy runners to move huge stone statues. Sleds remained an important form of transportation until the invention of the wheel and the axle. Today the transfer of goods by sleigh is limited to regions with very cold climates.

Homemade sleds built for recreational purposes may have existed in colonial America as early as the 1600s, but sleds were not made commercially in the United States until the 1870s. Early versions featured wooden or iron runners and could not be steered. Over the years, modifications were made in the design of runners to prevent the vehicle from sliding sideways, to protect drivers, and to improve steering.

Dogsleds. Peoples living in Canada, Alaska, Lapland, and northern Asia have relied on dogsleds for basic transportation over the snow-covered landscape for more than 1,000 years. Europeans who migrated to the coldest regions of North America adopted the dogsled as well, and it remained the only practical means of overland transportation until the invention of the snowmobile in the late 1950s. The first dogsled race was held in Alaska in 1908, and racing became a popular sport.

There are two basic types of Alaskan dogsleds—the Nome sledge and the Nansen sled. The Nome sledge has a long, narrow frame and can carry as much as 1,000 pounds (454 kg) of cargo. Nansen sleds, preferred by polar explorers of the past, are lighter and wider and have a load capacity of about 600 pounds (272 kg).

Usually either Siberian huskies or Alaskan malamutes are used to pull sleds. These large animals offer strength, endurance, and thick fur coats needed for the frigid north. The size of a team varies from several dogs to a dozen or more, depending on the weight of the load.

Recreational and Sport Sleds.
Coasting sleds, which are not pulled or dragged by animals, are used only for riding downhill. Models made of plastic or wood and steel are well suited to winter recreation. Toboggans and bobsleds compete in downhill races.

A full-size toboggan carries several racers seated one behind the other; the smaller luge toboggan, which has runners, holds one or two passengers. Bobsleds feature four runners mounted in two sets of two each. The front set can be turned to steer the vehicle as it hurtles down the slope. *See also* ANIMALS, PACK AND DRAFT; SNOWMOBILES.

Smuggling

customs tax on imported goods

Smuggling is the illegal, secret transportation of goods, usually across a national border. Smugglers may carry something that is legal in itself, such as tobacco, but hide it to avoid paying the necessary **customs.** Smugglers also may handle illegal goods such as narcotics, stolen property, and certain kinds of weapons.

The crime of smuggling has probably existed for as long as governments have tried to tax or regulate trade. Smugglers have used almost every form of transportation, from camel caravans to aircraft. One approach is to run goods across frontiers at isolated locations, hoping to avoid detection by law enforcement officials. The other approach is to hide items among cargoes, in baggage, or in vehicles that will cross borders openly at checkpoints.

Smuggled Goods.
Smugglers concentrate on items that are subject to high taxes or for which there is a great demand. When wars cut Great Britain off from trade with European merchants in the late 1700s and early 1800s, British smugglers found that they could obtain high prices for French brandy and lace. Smuggling became so widespread that the British government had to maintain a special fleet to catch smugglers in the English Channel.

A similar situation occurred when the United States temporarily outlawed liquor from 1920 to 1933. Boats called rumrunners brought alcohol from Europe and the West Indies to remote coves along the Atlantic coast, and trucks carried liquor across the Canadian border. In the latter half of the 1900s, smugglers worldwide turned to narcotics trafficking, with drugs such as marijuana, heroin, and cocaine. Valuable and easy to conceal, drugs are ideal items from a smuggler's point of view.

A variety of other products are trafficked illegally. Like drugs, precious stones are valuable and small. South Africa produces a large share of the world's diamonds and has strict antismuggling laws and procedures to combat the loss of gems from its mines. More difficult to smuggle, but sometimes quite profitable, is human cargo. After the slave trade was outlawed in Britain and the United States in the early 1800s, some ships smuggled African slaves. More recently, illegal immigrants have paid people to smuggle them into the United States.

Law Enforcement. Countries take various measures against smuggling. Some efforts are aimed at deterrence, or discouraging people from attempting to commit the crime. Others focus on interdiction—intercepting smuggled goods at the border—or on the identification and punishment of smugglers.

Legal entry into and departure from nations are regulated by customs agents, government officials who examine cargo, assess taxes, and search for contraband, or smuggled goods. They work with representatives of other law enforcement agencies. In the United States, these include the Federal Bureau of Investigation (FBI) and the Bureau of Alcohol, Tobacco, and Firearms (ATF). The U.S. Coast Guard was organized to fight smuggling and piracy, and the prevention of smuggling remains one of its chief tasks. The International Criminal Police Organization, known as Interpol, coordinates international antismuggling activities.
See also COAST GUARD; CRIME; CUSTOMS; PIRACY.

Snowmobiles

Snowmobiles are motorized vehicles that provide transportation over snow or ice. They have largely replaced dogsleds as the basic means of travel in northern regions and are popular with winter sports enthusiasts.

In the 1920s a Wisconsin storekeeper built a sled that was powered by an airplane propeller and steered with skis. This early version of the snowmobile was large, slow, and difficult to operate. In 1958 a Canadian

Snowmobiles provide transportation in northern regions where the land is covered with snow or ice. The snowmobile shown is on Ross Island, Antarctica.

inventor named Joseph-Armand Bombardier developed a smaller, lighter version of the motorized sled called the Ski-Dog. The following year Bombardier redesigned the vehicle and reintroduced it as the Ski-Doo. Since that time, the basic design of snowmobiles has changed little.

Equipped with a gasoline engine ranging from 8 to 100 horsepower, snowmobiles can reach speeds of more than 100 miles per hour (161 km per hour). They feature two short skis in front and a rotating rubber track in the rear that propels the vehicle across the snow or ice. The driver steers the vehicle with handlebars and controls its speed with a throttle and a brake.

After the introduction of the Ski-Doo, snowmobiling grew rapidly as a sport, especially in the northern United States, Canada, and Europe. Snowmobiles also have practical applications. They allow people in northern regions to travel and carry goods to areas that cannot be reached by other forms of ground transportation in winter. *See also* SLEIGHS.

Snowshoes

Snowshoes are devices that help people travel across soft or deep snow. The wearer straps the flat frames, which measure at least 3 feet (1 m) long and 1½ feet (46 cm) wide, to boots or shoes. By spreading the body's weight over a larger area, snowshoes enable an individual to walk or run without sinking into the snow.

Native Americans and early settlers in snowy parts of North America used snowshoes made of wooden hoops crisscrossed with strips of animal hide. Although some companies still manufacture wood and leather snowshoes, today most are made of strong plastics and lightweight metals such as titanium. Many models have spikes on their undersides for better traction on slick or steep surfaces. Oval, or bear paw, snowshoes are well suited to rough terrain; long, narrow shoes with "tails" are best for open areas and racing. Some manufacturers produce small, lightweight snowshoes especially designed for women and children.

Hunters, trappers, and forest workers have long used snowshoes. Snowshoeing has also gained popularity as a winter sport, leading to special clubs, classes, and races across North America. *See also* SPORTS AND RECREATION.

Sonar

Sonar is a system for detecting sounds and objects underwater. Its name comes from the initial letters of the words *sound navigation and ranging.*

The two main types of sonar are active sonar and passive sonar. Active sonar uses a device called a transducer to convert electrical currents into sound waves. The sound waves travel through water, and when they strike a solid object, they are reflected back toward the transducer. The reflected waves and the time of their return provide information, which may be displayed on a screen or other device, about the object's location, distance, and direction of movement. Passive sonar does not transmit sound but picks up the noise produced by underwater objects.

During World War I, American and British scientists tried to develop a system that could locate enemy submarines. They experimented with towing microphones behind ships, but they did not create true active and passive sonar systems until the 1920s. Kept secret, sonar later helped the Allies during World War II.

Since the mid-1940s, sonar has increased in accuracy and range. It continues to serve ships as they navigate in unfamiliar waters or hunt for submarines and mines. Sonar's nonmilitary functions include locating schools of fish, mapping the ocean floor, and salvaging shipwrecks. Sonar systems may be carried by ships, submarines, and airplanes and mounted on **buoys.** *See also* NAVIGATION; SHIPWRECKS; SIGNALING.

buoy floating marker in the water

Songs

Travel and transportation have inspired many types of songs over the years. Sailors sang to keep in rhythm as they toiled together on long, difficult voyages. Pioneers settling in unfamiliar lands often sang of their suffering, loneliness, and hope for a new life. Others created songs describing the hardships and rewards of travel. Although such music certainly formed part of many cultural traditions, American folk music includes an especially rich selection of these songs.

Songs from the Sea. There are two main categories of sea songs. One consists of chanteys (sometimes spelled "shanties"), or work songs. The other includes songs that sailors used to entertain one another, sometimes called fo'c'sle songs. (Fo'c'sle refers to the forecastle, a region in the bow of a ship where sailors slept and spent their leisure time.) Both types of songs have existed for centuries, but many of those that were written down date from the mid-1800s, when large American ships traveled the seas in great numbers.

Chanteys were less concerned with the words than the rhythm, which was meant to keep a crew working in time as they performed such grueling duties as heaving the anchor or pumping water out of the vessel. Many such songs contained directions, as in these lines from "South Australia":

> In South Austraylia I was born,
> Heave away, haul away,
> In South Austraylia I was born,
> Heave away your rolling chain
> We're bound for South Austraylia.

Fishing, riverboating, and other methods of seafaring also inspired sailors to sing. The Erie Canal and the Great Lakes both gave rise to a collection of songs. The author of "The Raging Canawl" warns others about the dangers of sailing on the canal:

> Come, listen to my story, ye landsmen, one and all,
> And I'll sing to you the dangers of that raging canal;
> For I am one of many who expects a watery grave,
> For I've been at the mercies of the winds and the waves.

In the late 1800s steam replaced sails on ships, reducing the size of the crew needed to keep a vessel afloat. As a result, chanteys became little more than a curiosity of **maritime** history. Nevertheless, in the

All in a Day's Work

In the decades after the Civil War, cowboys drove large herds of young cattle along trails from Texas to markets in the north, where they would be sold for beef. "Whoopee, Ti Yi Yo, Git Along, Little Dogies," a song made popular on the prairies of the West, describes the way that the cowboys prodded the cattle to continue moving on the trail:

> It's whooping and yelling and
>   driving the dogies;
> O how I wish they would go on!
> It's whooping and punching and
>   go on little dogies,
> For you know Wyoming will be
>   your new home.

maritime related to the sea or shipping

As pioneers journeyed westward crossing open prairies in wagon trains, they often sang songs about the hardships of frontier life and their hopes for the future.

West Indies, where sailing ships are still used for travel among the islands, many traditional sea songs survive with local words and place names.

Travelers on Land. Singing was one of the few amusements available to pioneers who settled the western part of the United States. Many of their songs deal with the conditions of frontier living. For example, "The Little Old Sod Shanty" offers a humorous look at the lonely, uncomfortable life of a bachelor in his prairie home. "Sweet Betsy from Pike" tells of the adventures of a couple crossing the West to reach the California goldfields.

By the late 1800s, hoboes, young men who wandered from place to place in search of work, were becoming part of the American landscape. When work ran out, they lived on handouts from individuals or local groups. Hoboes' songs reflect both good humor and underlying bitterness, as in this verse from "Hallelujah, I'm a Bum!":

> I went to a house,
> And I asked for a piece of bread;
> A lady came out, says,
> "The baker is dead."

Some folk songs drew on the feelings people had about the magnificent yet lonely countryside and the uncertain lifestyles that many led there. "The Dreary Black Hills" tells of a prospector's failure to find gold in Wyoming, and "Dakota Land" describes the harshness of the northern plains. Cowboy songs such as "The Lone Star Trail" reflect experiences on the cattle trails of the Old West.

The building of the railroads in the mid-1800s led to new songs. Some of them, like sea chanteys, were sung by work gangs. Other songs marked events, honored individuals, or celebrated the experience of train travel. "Poor Paddy Works on the Railway" was an anthem for the Irish workers who wielded picks and shovels in the building of the railways. "The Railroad Cars Are Coming" captures the excitement people felt as this new form of transportation began to transform the West:

> The great Pacific railway,
> For California hail!
> Bring on the locomotive,
> Lay down the iron rail.

See also HOBOES; LITERATURE.

Soyuz Spacecraft

Soviet Union *nation that existed from 1922 to 1991, made up of Russia and 14 other republics in eastern Europe and northern Asia*

cosmonaut *Russian term for a person who travels into space; literally "traveler to the universe"*

Since 1967 the **Soviet Union** and Russia have launched a series of crewed and uncrewed spacecraft called Soyuz (which means "union" in Russian). Soyuz contained three modules, or sections: an instrument module that held the rocket motors, equipment, and fuel; an orbital module that served as a work center for the **cosmonauts;** and a reentry module for bringing the crew back to Earth. Before the spacecraft returned from space, the reentry module separated from the other modules. The speed of its reentry was slowed first by the Earth's atmosphere, then by parachutes, and finally by rockets just before landing. Unlike American space capsules that land in the ocean, Soyuz was designed to touch down on the ground.

Launched on April 23, 1967, the first Soyuz met a tragic end when its parachutes failed to open properly, killing cosmonaut Vladimir Komarov. In January 1969 the Soviets succeeded in linking *Soyuz 4* and *Soyuz 5* in space. During the mission, crew members from one craft moved to the other for the first time. The following year, two cosmonauts set a record by spending 18 days in orbit aboard *Soyuz 9*. After this mission, Soyuz was modified to transport crews to and from the new Salyut space station.

A second disaster occurred in June 1971, when a valve on *Soyuz 11* opened during reentry and the air escaped from the cabin. Because the craft was too small to allow the cosmonauts to wear space suits, all three crew members suffocated. Soyuz was remodeled to accommodate two cosmonauts wearing space suits, and missions to the space station resumed. In July 1975 *Soyuz 19* made history when it docked with an American Apollo capsule and the two craft remained together for 47 hours. This was the first joint space flight between the United States and the Soviet Union.

In December 1979, the *Soyuz T* (Transport) was introduced. Featuring advanced electronics and navigational capabilities, the craft could hold three cosmonauts in space suits and used a new reentry procedure that consumed less fuel. *Soyuz T* flights continued until the development in 1986 of *Soyuz TM*, the spacecraft designed to carry crews to and from the *Mir* space station. *See also* COSMONAUTS; MIR; SALYUT SPACE STATIONS; SPACE EXPLORATION; SPACE SUITS; SPACE TRAVEL.

Spacecraft, Parts of

propulsion *process of driving or propelling*

All vehicles—from sailing ships to spacecraft—must be designed to carry people safely and efficiently. But spacecraft must also provide the equipment, supplies, and controlled environment needed to survive in space. Even the most basic elements of transportation—such as **propulsion**, navigation, and communication—are far more complex on a spacecraft than they are for other vehicles.

Spacecraft come in a variety of forms and have different parts and equipment to perform particular functions. Yet all contain certain basic systems. These include a propulsion system—some sort of rocket—to lift the vehicle into and beyond Earth's orbit. Every spacecraft also needs a direction and navigation system to guide the craft toward a destination; a power system to provide energy for onboard operations; and a communication system for contact with control centers on Earth. Spacecraft that carry passengers must provide a suitable environment for humans.

Propulsion Systems

There are two types of propulsion systems used to launch spacecraft and move them through space. External propulsion systems, large rockets attached to the craft, provide the power needed for launching. Internal propulsion systems, located aboard the spacecraft, allow the vehicle to speed up or slow down during its journey.

Rockets. A rocket is a tube filled with fuel and an oxidizer—a substance that provides the oxygen needed to burn fuel in the airless void of space. When mixed and ignited, the fuel and oxidizer burn and produce rapidly expanding gases. These gases are directed out an opening at one end of the rocket, providing the thrust needed to propel the rocket into space.

There are two main types of rockets: solid-fuel and liquid-fuel rockets. Solid-fuel rockets are simple and inexpensive to build. The burning of solid fuel, however, cannot be controlled, nor can the rocket be stopped and started again once the fuel has been ignited. Most spacecraft are launched by liquid-fuel rockets, which produce a great deal of energy relative to their weight. In addition, liquid-fuel rockets can be stopped and restarted as necessary, and the rate at which the fuel burns can be controlled.

Nuclear-propelled rockets have gone through a series of testing. They proved to be efficient and more economical than standard rockets, but concerns about their safety and the effect on the environment have prevented their use in launching spacecraft.

Parts of a Space Shuttle Orbiter

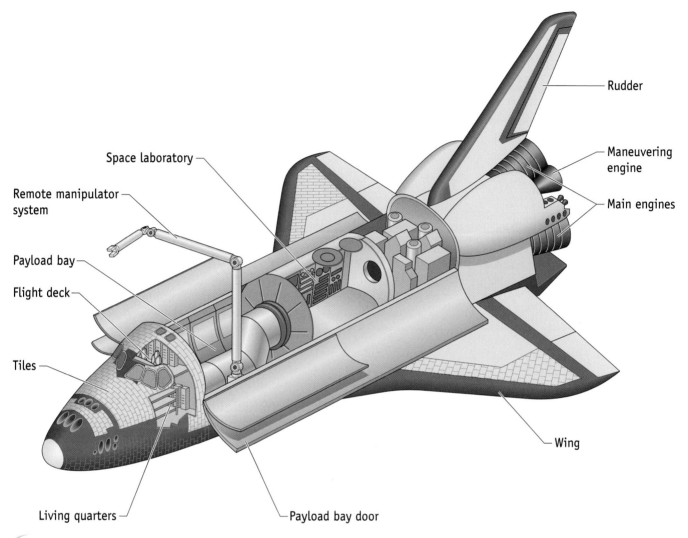

Rudder

Maneuvering engine

Main engines

Space laboratory

Remote manipulator system

Payload bay

Flight deck

Tiles

Wing

Living quarters

Payload bay door

This drawing shows the main parts of a space shuttle orbiter.

Most rockets used to launch spacecraft consist of three or four stages—separate rockets stacked on top of one another. When the fuel in one stage is used up, the stage separates and falls away, and the next stage ignites. As each stage drops off, the rocket becomes lighter. At the same time, the pull of gravity becomes weaker as the rocket rises higher into space. Consequently, the rocket continues to accelerate throughout its flight.

maneuver to make a series of changes in course

Internal Propulsion. Most spacecraft carry very little fuel. The launch rocket pushes the vehicle toward its target, and the vehicle basically coasts to its destination. However, if a spacecraft needs to speed up, slow down, or **maneuver,** it uses its internal propulsion system. These systems run on liquid fuel, which allows the rate of burning to be controlled.

lunar referring to the Moon

Most piloted spacecraft contain small rocket engines on board. The Apollo spacecraft that went to the Moon activated its internal rockets to break free of the **lunar** orbit and return to Earth. Some orbiting spacecraft use internal rockets called retro rockets to slow down, allowing

51

them to fall out of orbit and reenter Earth's atmosphere. The space shuttle has internal rocket engines that enable it to maneuver in space and return to Earth.

Scientists are experimenting with new types of internal propulsion systems. The ion-propulsion engine, for example, works by removing tiny, negatively charged particles called ions from a fuel such as mercury or even water. A strong magnetic field acts on the remaining positively charged ions to produce thrust. Though not powerful enough to launch a spacecraft, ion engines could be used for internal propulsion on long space flights.

Direction and Navigation Systems

The path of a spacecraft is usually calculated and entered in an onboard computer before liftoff. However, navigating in space can be tricky, and course changes or adjustments often must be made during flight. Various systems on the spacecraft keep track of its position in space and make adjustments to its course.

Attitude Control.
Attitude refers to a vehicle's orientation in space. Spacecraft often have small liquid-fuel rockets or jets using pressurized gas that enable them to adjust their attitude. With these systems, a vehicle can change its movement from side to side (called yaw), raise or lower its nose (called pitch), or rotate around its axis (called roll).

Navigation.
A spacecraft never travels in a straight line or at a constant speed because many different forces affect its movement. But correcting the position and direction of the craft is difficult for there are no fixed landmarks in space. For this reason, vehicles must navigate by other means such as an internal guidance system.

The internal guidance system of a spacecraft includes gyroscopes—devices that spin at a constant speed regardless of the movement of the spacecraft—and accelerometers, instruments that measure the forward motion of the vehicle. Computers constantly monitor these devices to detect any changes in direction or speed, and they analyze the data to determine the location of the spacecraft at any time in its flight.

If a spacecraft goes off course, the rocket engines of its internal propulsion system are fired to put the vehicle back on track. On a piloted spacecraft, the crew often carries out this task. On a space **probe** or other uncrewed satellite, the commands are executed by computers either on the spacecraft or on Earth.

probe uncrewed spacecraft sent out to explore and collect information in space

Power Systems

A spacecraft contains a great deal of equipment that requires electrical power to operate. This power may be provided by various methods, including the use of solar cells, special long-lasting batteries, and nuclear generators.

Solar Cells and Batteries.

Spacecraft traveling in the inner regions of our solar system are close enough to the Sun to use its energy as a source of power. Solar cells—also called photovoltaic cells—collect energy from the Sun and convert it into electricity.

Solar cells are the primary source of power for most artificial satellites, space stations, and space probes that operate close to the Sun. The surfaces of some satellites are completely covered with such cells, allowing them to receive a constant supply of solar energy no matter what direction they are facing. On other satellites and most larger spacecraft, solar cells take the form of large, flat panels that must be adjusted periodically to face the Sun and collect its energy.

Energy collected by solar cells but not used immediately may be stored in special long-lasting batteries made of either nickel and cadmium or nickel and hydrogen. Some batteries can last for ten years or longer. Small satellites and space probes that do not require large amounts of energy often use batteries as their source of power.

Nuclear Generators.

Space probes and other craft that travel to the far reaches of the solar system are too far from the Sun to collect enough solar energy to provide them with power. Such spacecraft contain a tiny amount of radioactive material that produces heat as it decays. A nuclear generator transforms that heat into electrical power for the systems aboard the spacecraft.

In this photo, technicians work on Galileo, the Jupiter probe, at NASA's Jet Propulsion Lab in California.

Environment and Life-Support Systems

Spacecraft that carry humans must have systems to provide a safe environment and the basic elements of life support, such as oxygen and water. Even uncrewed spacecraft must be built in a way that protects their instruments from the hazards of space.

radiation tiny, harmful particles of matter given off during a nuclear reaction

Environment. Space is a very hostile environment for both humans and machines. Spacecraft are subjected to temperatures and pressures much more extreme than those found on Earth. They are also exposed to **radiation** that can harm humans and damage sensitive instruments. Even small dust particles moving through space at tremendous speeds can pose a danger to humans and equipment.

Spacecraft are designed with several features to protect their crew and cargo from such dangers. They have special coatings and insulation that help keep temperatures inside within a safe range. Piloted vehicles are equipped with temperature-control systems that maintain the interior at a comfortable level for the crew.

Many spacecraft have special shielding to protect against various forms of radiation as well as meteorites and other particles in space. Ultraviolet radiation emitted by the Sun can damage human eyes and cause some materials such as rubber and plastic to break down. Special filters on the windows of spacecraft reduce ultraviolet radiation.

friction force that produces a resistance to motion

Spacecraft must not only withstand the environment of space, they must also be able to resist the tremendous stresses of liftoff and reentry into Earth's atmosphere. Reentry poses a specific set of problems, including the extremely high temperatures caused by **friction** as the spacecraft moves at very high speeds. Early space capsules had heat shields to absorb and radiate away the heat of reentry. Most of these early shields burned up and disintegrated as they absorbed heat. When reusable spacecraft, such as the space shuttle, were developed, they needed a heat protection system that could also be reused.

Scientists solved this problem with special ceramic-coated tiles made of silica and carbon to absorb heat. The space shuttle contains more than 25,000 of these tiles, which are individually shaped and placed on its underside, nose, and front edges of the tail and wings. The tiles are so efficient at absorbing and radiating heat that they can withstand temperatures in excess of 3,000°F (1,650°C).

Life Support. Humans must carry their own food, water, and oxygen supplies to survive in space. However, the restricted storage space on a spacecraft severely limits the amount that can be brought. Fresh air for the crew is supplied by tanks containing oxygen and other gases. Most piloted spacecraft also contain devices that can recycle the carbon dioxide exhaled by crew members and convert it into usable oxygen.

The spacecraft carries tanks that hold water for drinking and other uses. In addition, water is recycled by systems that collect moisture from breathing, sweating, and urination. Some of the recycled water is purified for drinking; some is used only for washing. Food is the only essential life-support element that cannot yet be produced in space, so a crew must carry all the food it will need for a mission. Scientists are working to develop ways to produce plant foods onboard a spacecraft during long voyages.

Communications and Tracking

Ground-control crews need to keep in touch with a spacecraft and track its progress during a mission. These tasks are carried out by systems both on Earth and onboard the spacecraft.

All spacecraft contain radios with which to send and receive signals. Piloted spacecraft have voice radio as well. Spacecraft are also equipped with telemetry, an electronic system that makes measurements and observations and relays the data to Earth by radio signals. Telemetry provides a continually updated report on the condition of the spacecraft—its temperature, the levels of radiation to which it is exposed, and the performance of its systems. In addition, spacecraft use telemetry to transmit information gathered by their instruments and even photos. The radio signals received by communication centers on Earth are decoded by computers and put into a form that can be understood by flight technicians. Ground crews also use telemetry to send commands and computer programs to unpiloted spacecraft.

The flight of a spacecraft is tracked on Earth by a network of communication stations, tracking antennae, and satellites. The communication stations send the information they receive to facilities in centralized locations, where ground crews monitor the progress of the flight.

Scientific Instrumentation

All spacecraft carry various types of scientific instruments to make measurements and observations and to accomplish the tasks for which the spacecraft was designed. Communications satellites have devices called transponders, which receive television or radio signals, amplify them, and transmit them to Earth. Some satellites carry special cameras to observe and photograph the Earth, while others have devices to monitor weather conditions on the planet.

Orbiting space telescopes give astronomers a clearer view of deep space. Space probes carry equipment to measure such things as a planet's magnetic field and the composition of its atmosphere. They also have cameras and telescopes to take photos of planets, comets, and asteroids. Probes that land on the Moon and other planets may have mechanical arms to sample rocks and soil, and onboard laboratories to analyze the material that is collected.

Piloted spacecraft carry equipment to perform experiments in the weightless environment of space or to take measurements outside the Earth's atmosphere. The space shuttle can transport Spacelab, a self-contained scientific laboratory. Space stations have additional room for

Keeping Clean in Space

A special challenge for crews on long space flights is keeping clean. Early vehicles were much too small, and their missions too short, to include washing facilities. However, space stations may have astronauts in residence for several months. The U.S. space station *Skylab* had a collapsible shower stall that allowed crew members to bathe. After showering, astronauts had to vacuum up the remaining water droplets or they would float around inside the spacecraft. The Soviet space station *Mir* was also equipped with a shower. Astronauts on the U.S. space shuttle have to settle for sponge baths.

scientific equipment to gather data and for astronauts to carry out experiments. *See also* GYROSCOPE; ROCKETS; SATELLITES; SPACE EXPLORATION; SPACE PROBES; SPACE ROVERS; SPACE SHUTTLES; SPACE STATIONS; SPACE SUITS; SPACE TRAVEL.

Space Exploration

Further Information
To learn more about space exploration, including space agencies, mission programs, individuals who have played a role in space exploration, and different types of spacecraft, see the related articles listed at the end of this entry.

The story of space exploration is a tale of impossible dreamers, human courage, international rivalry, and the perseverance of those who believed that they could one day reach the stars. The space age began in 1957 with the launching of *Sputnik 1,* the world's first artificial satellite. Although primitive by today's standards, the satellite represented a momentous technological achievement. Just 30 years earlier, space exploration was considered impossible by all but a handful of visionaries. By the year 2000, humans had landed on the Moon and launched spacecraft to explore nearly all of the other planets in the solar system.

Pioneers of Space

Many ancient peoples studied the night skies, and some even dreamed of travel to other worlds. In the A.D. 100s, the Greek orator Lucian wrote the oldest recorded story of a trip to the Moon. Despite careful observation, however, it was not until the invention of the telescope in the early 1600s that humans began to understand more fully the lights they saw in the sky.

Early Astronomers. The first person to use a telescope to study the heavens was Italian scientist Galileo Galilei in the early 1600s. On the basis of his observations, Galileo mapped the Moon's surface, noting its mountains and valleys. He also discovered several moons orbiting the planet Jupiter.

Galileo's observations were soon followed by the work of other scientists. German astronomer Johannes Kepler determined that planetary orbits were elliptical, or oval, rather than circular. Kepler was also the first scientist to describe space travel.

In the late 1600s English scientist Sir Isaac Newton built on earlier knowledge to formulate laws of motion. Newton's laws allowed space pioneers nearly 300 years later to determine the kinds of flight paths that would enable them to escape Earth's gravity, reach orbit above the planet, and ultimately travel into outer space.

Rocket Pioneers. By the early 1900s airplanes had made powered flight a reality, but the idea of space flight was still a fantasy. However, in 1903 a Russian teacher named Konstantin Tsiolkovsky published the first scientific paper on rocket-powered space flight. Tsiolkovsky proposed using liquid forms of hydrogen and oxygen as rocket fuels. Like the ideas of many pioneers, Tsiolkovsky's work was little understood or appreciated at the time.

In the 1920s American scientist Robert Goddard began experimenting with rocket motors and **propellants.** By 1926 he had launched the

propellant fuel

Major Events in Space Exploration

Date	Program	Crew	Mission
October 1957	Sputnick 1		First artificial satellite to orbit the Earth
January 1958	Explorer 1		First American artificial satellite
January 1959	Luna 1		First spacecraft to pass near the Moon
April 1961	Vostok 1	Yuri Gagarin	First human in space
May 1961	Mercury 3	Alan Shepard	First American in space
February 1962	Mercury 6	John Glenn	First American to orbit the Earth
June 1963	Vostok 6	Valentina Tereshkova	First woman in space
March 1965	Voshkod 2	Alexei Leonov, Pavel Belayev	First space walk
June 1965	Gemini 4	Edward White II, James McDivitt	First American space walk
December 1968	Apollo 8	Frank Borman, James Lovell Jr. William Anders	First humans to orbit the Moon
July 1969	Apollo 11	Neil Armstrong, Edwin E. Aldrin Jr. Michael Collins	First human landing on the Moon
December 1970	Venera 7		First probe to land on Venus
April 1971	Salyut 1		First space station launched into orbit
June 1971	Soyuz 11	Georgi Dobrovolksy, Viktor Patsayev Vladislav Volkov	Spacecraft docked with Salyut space station
May 1973	Skylab 1		First U.S. space station
December 1973	Mariner 10		Probe that explored Venus and Mercury
July 1975	Soyuz 19 Apollo 18	Alexi Leonov, Valeri Kubasov Thomas Stafford, Donald Slayton Vance Brand	Apollo-Soyuz docking mission; first joint U.S.– Soviet Union mission
August 1977	Voyager 2		Sent images back to Earth of Jupiter (1979), Saturn (1981), Uranus (1986), and Neptune (1989)
April 1981	Columbia	John Young, Robert Crippen	First orbital flight of a U.S. space shuttle
June 1983	Challenger	Sally Ride, Robert Crippen Frederick Hauck, John Fabian Norman Thagard	First American woman in space
February 1986	Mir		Soviet space station launched
March 1986	Soyuz T15	Leonid Kizim, Vladimir Solovyev	First flight to Mir
April 1990	Discovery	Loren Shriver, Charles Bolden Steven Hawley, Bruce McCandless II Kathryn Sullivan	Launched the Hubble Space Telescope
October 1990	Ulysses		Joint ESA and NASA probe launched by space shuttle Discovery to orbit the Sun
June 1993	Endeavour	Ronald Grabe, Brian Duffy Donald Low, Jane Sherlock Janice Voss, Peter Wisoff	First flight of Spacelab to conduct experiments
July 1997	Mars Pathfinder		Probe that landed on Mars and sent images back to Earth
October 1998	Discovery	John Glenn, Stephen Robinson Curtis Brown Jr., Steven Lindsey Scott Parazynski, Pedro Duque Chiaki Mukai	Conducted experiments on the effects of space travel on the elderly
November 1998	International Space Station		First section of the International Space Station sent into orbit
May 1999	Discovery	Kent Rominger, Valery Tokarev Julie Payette, Rick Husbard Tammy Jernigan, Daniel Barry	First space shuttle to dock with the International Space Station

Soviet Union   International   United States

guided missile missile, or rocket, steered by radio signals and electronic codes

Soviet Union nation that existed from 1922 to 1991, made up of Russia and 14 other republics in eastern Europe and northern Asia.

world's first liquid-fuel rocket. Also in the 1920s, German scientist Hermann Oberth published two books discussing space travel, including multistage rockets and Earth-observing satellites. Oberth's ideas attracted the attention of the German government. During World War II German engineers, led by Wernher von Braun, developed the V-2 rocket, the world's first long-range **guided missile.**

Post-war Developments. After World War II many German rocket engineers moved to the United States or the **Soviet Union,** contributing to the development of rocket technology in those two countries. Both nations were exploring the use of rockets to carry explosive warheads long distances.

In the late 1940s some scientists in the United States wanted to study the possibility of launching an artificial satellite. But military officials rejected the idea because they thought such satellites had no scientific or military value. Nevertheless, a group of engineers including von Braun continued working on rocket and satellite technology. Their research led to the development in 1954 of Project Orbiter, a program aimed at sending a satellite into orbit atop a U.S. Army intermediate-range guided missile.

Rocket scientists got a boost that same year with the announcement of plans for an International Geophysical Year (IGY) in 1957 and 1958. The goals of the IGY were to coordinate research in all scientific fields in order to better understand Earth. The planners of IGY noted that an artificial satellite would be a helpful addition to the program, and both the United States and the Soviet Union announced plans to launch a satellite during the IGY.

It was widely assumed at the time that U.S. technology was far superior to that of the Soviets and that the United States would launch a satellite first. But the Soviets had been developing larger and more powerful rockets than the United States. While the United States struggled to develop a rocket capable of carrying a satellite into space, the Soviets stunned the world by sending *Sputnik 1* into orbit around the Earth on October 4, 1957.

The successful launching of *Sputnik 1* surprised and worried people in the United States, and the U.S. government stepped up efforts in rocket and space technology. For the next decade or more the United States and the Soviet Union engaged in a race to improve space flight and gain the lead in space exploration and travel.

The Soviet Space Program

The Soviet Union quickly extended its lead over the United States. In November 1957 it launched *Sputnik 2,* which carried a dog named Laika. The flight proved that animals could survive in space and was considered the first step toward a space mission with a human passenger. In May 1958 a third Sputnik was launched into orbit around the Earth, where it performed scientific experiments for two years. The following January the Soviet **probe** *Luna 1* became the first spacecraft to pass near the Moon. As impressive as these feats were, the Soviet

probe spacecraft sent out to explore and collect information in space

Union was focused on a more ambitious goal—sending the first human into space.

cosmonaut Russian term for a person who travels into space; literally, "traveler to the universe"

Series of "Firsts."

On April 12, 1961, Soviet **cosmonaut** Yuri Gagarin circled the Earth once in a spacecraft named *Vostok 1,* becoming the first person to leave Earth's atmosphere and enter outer space. Once again, the Soviet Union had beaten the United States to a major milestone in space exploration.

Vostok 2 followed in August 1961, making 17 orbits before returning safely to Earth. The next year *Vostok 3* and *Vostok 4* were launched a day apart and passed close by each other in orbit, as did *Vostok 5* and *Vostok 6* in June 1963. *Vostok 6* was piloted by Valentina Tereshkova, the first woman in space.

In October 1964 the Soviet Union launched the first of a series of spacecraft called Voshkod. The Voshkod spacecraft, which had room for three cosmonauts, were the first ones capable of carrying more than one person.

Voshkod 2, launched in March 1965, featured the first space walk, as cosmonaut Alexei Leonov left the spacecraft for a brief time. The Vostok and Voshkod flights were highly successful. But the next space program, called Soyuz, surpassed them in both length of time and achievements in space.

Success and Failure.

Soyuz 1, the largest and most complex spacecraft yet developed by the Soviet Union, was launched in April 1967, two years after the last Voshkod flight. The mission had a tragic ending. A parachute failed to work properly during reentry and the spacecraft crashed, killing cosmonaut Vladimir Komarov. His death was the first resulting from a space flight.

The *Soyuz 1* accident set the Soviet crewed space program back about 18 months. But in 1968 an improved version of the Soyuz spacecraft was launched and recovered without difficulty. Over the next year and a half, six more Soyuz spacecraft orbited the Earth. *Soyuz 9* stayed in orbit nearly 18 days, a record at that time.

By the mid-1960s the United States was working on a highly publicized effort to put a human on the Moon. Although at the time the Soviets denied having a similar goal, information released more than 20 years later showed that they had tried to reach the Moon and failed. The Soviet program, called Zond, suffered repeated setbacks such as rockets exploding during testing.

Space Stations.

Despite the failure of their Moon program, the Soviets made great strides in other areas of space exploration. In April 1971 they placed the first space station in orbit around Earth. Called *Salyut 1,* the station was a single module, or unit, that could accommodate three cosmonauts and had a docking port for one spacecraft. The Salyut space station had a difficult start. The first crew of cosmonauts in the station spent 24 days there, proving that extended stays in space were possible. But while returning to Earth, a malfunction in their Soyuz spacecraft caused the air supply to leak out, killing all three men.

Alan Shepard became the first American to be sent into space in May 1961. At the end of his flight in the Freedom 7 space capsule, he splashed down in the Atlantic Ocean and boarded a rescue helicopter.

Between 1971 and 1986 the Soviets placed several other Salyut space stations in orbit, each an improvement over the last. *Salyut 6,* launched in 1977, had docking ports for two spacecraft. This new design allowed the station crews to receive visitors and supplies from other spacecraft, enabling them to remain at the station for long periods. The space station was replaced in 1982 by *Salyut 7,* which remained in operation until 1986.

In 1986 the Soviets launched a more elaborate space station called *Mir.* The main section of *Mir* was launched first, and three laboratory modules were sent up later and docked with the core module. *Mir* was almost continuously occupied by cosmonauts (joined on later missions by American astronauts) from 1986 to 1999. One cosmonaut crew stayed aboard the station for an entire year.

Space Probes. Although crewed flights played a central role in the Soviet space program, the nation also launched many unpiloted space probes. The goal was to explore the Moon and planets and gather important scientific information there.

Starting in 1959 the Soviets launched a series of **lunar** probes. Among the major achievements of the program were *Luna 2* (1959), the first spacecraft to touch the Moon's surface, and *Luna 9* (1966), the first spacecraft to land on the Moon and transmit pictures. Later in 1966, *Luna 10* succeeded in orbiting the Moon. By 1976 a total of 24 Luna probes had been launched, sending photos and scientific data from the Moon.

lunar referring to the Moon

The Soviets also made extensive efforts to explore Venus and Mars with space probes. *Venera 3* entered the atmosphere of Venus on March 1, 1966, becoming the first humanmade vehicle to reach another planet. The probe's communication system failed, however, as it neared Venus. *Venera 4,* launched in June 1967, separated into two sections on reaching Venus. One section entered the planet's atmosphere, while the other transmitted information about Venus to Earth. Neither section of the probe reached the surface of Venus. That feat was accomplished in December 1970 by *Venera 7,* the first probe to land on the surface of another planet. The probe sent back readings of temperatures of more than 880°F (471°C) on Venus and **atmospheric pressure** 90 times greater than that at sea level on Earth. In 1975 *Venera 9* and *Venera 10* transmitted the first pictures from Venus. Eight years later *Venera 15* and *Venera 16* orbited the planet and used radar to produce maps of the surface.

atmospheric pressure pressure exerted by the Earth's atmosphere at any given point on the planet's surface

The Mars program was much less successful. In 1962 the first Soviet probe, *Mars 1,* lost contact with Earth after a flight of some 7 million miles (11 million km). The next six probes all reached the planet, but only two—*Mars 3* and *Mars 5*—transmitted back useful information or photographs.

The U.S. Space Program

While the Soviet space program began with great flourish, the United States stumbled badly in its early efforts. The first U.S. space program, called Vanguard, lacked adequate funding and suffered many technical and other problems. Five of the first six rocket boosters exploded on the launching pad, and the first successful launch of a Vanguard satellite did not take place until March 1958, over four months after *Sputnik 1.*

Explorer and NASA.

Vanguard was not even the first American satellite in space. That honor went to *Explorer 1,* which was launched in January 1958 aboard a Jupiter-C rocket. *Sputnik 1* reached space first, but *Explorer 1* proved to be more useful as a scientific tool. While orbiting Earth, it found an area of intense radiation surrounding the planet. This zone was named the Van Allen belts after one of the scientists who worked on *Explorer 1.* The discovery of the Van Allen belts was considered one of the most important developments of the International Geophysical Year.

Despite this achievement, it was clear that the United States still lagged behind the Soviets in space. In 1958 the U.S. government created an agency to oversee the nation's civilian space program. Called the National Aeronautics and Space Administration (NASA), it helped coordinate the many separate projects in the U.S. space program at the time. Many experts believe that the creation of NASA was the single biggest factor that led to eventual American superiority in space.

Early Crewed Space Missions.

The U.S. program aimed at putting a human in space was called Project Mercury. Its first mission took place on May 5, 1961, when astronaut Alan Shepard completed a 15-minute **suborbital** flight aboard a space capsule named *Freedom 7.*

suborbital refers to flight into space that does not go into orbit

No American orbited the Earth until February 20, 1962, when John Glenn was sent into space aboard *Friendship 7* and circled Earth three times. The United States launched three more Mercury flights in 1962 and 1963. In the final Mercury mission in May 1963, astronaut L. Gordon Cooper remained in space one and a half days before returning safely to Earth.

Project Mercury was followed by Project Gemini, a series of two-person flights intended to serve as a testing ground for tasks such as **maneuvering** and docking in space. Another purpose of Project Gemini was to study the effects on humans of such phenomena as long-term weightlessness and the reactions of astronauts during complex and difficult tasks. The ultimate goal of Gemini was to work out many of the problems that needed to be solved in order to land a person on the Moon.

maneuver to make a series of changes in course

The first American space walk—by astronaut Edward H. White II—took place in June 1965 on *Gemini 4.* Two months later the *Gemini 5* astronauts set a record by spending nearly eight days in space. *Gemini 6* and *Gemini 7,* launched in December 1965, featured the first close rendezvous of two spacecraft, which orbited Earth together for several hours.

The first successful docking of two spacecraft took place in March 1966, with the linkup of *Gemini 8* and an unpiloted Agena rocket. This mission almost ended in tragedy when the two vehicles began to tumble out of control. But the astronauts regained control and landed safely. A total of ten piloted Gemini flights provided experience and information that proved invaluable for a mission to the Moon.

The space shuttle is used for research as well as for transportation. Crew members conduct experiments in the shuttle's science module, shown here.

The Apollo Program. While Project Gemini was solving practical problems, American engineers and scientists were busy designing the rockets and vehicles needed for Apollo, a lunar mission. The project had the support of President Kennedy, who had asked NASA to work toward the goal of landing astronauts on the Moon before the end of the 1960s.

One of the greatest challenges of the Apollo program was developing a rocket powerful enough to escape Earth's gravity. Launching a small lunar probe was one thing; launching three astronauts and all the equipment and vehicles needed to take them to the Moon and back was quite another. The solution was the Saturn V, the most powerful rocket ever designed. But when the Apollo program began, the Saturn V was far from ready.

Scientists and engineers at NASA had the challenge of designing a spacecraft that would take the astronauts to the Moon, land them on its surface, and return them safely to Earth. They decided on a vehicle with two sections: a lunar module (LM) and a combined command/service module (CSM). The CSM would travel from Earth to the Moon with the LM and remain in orbit around the Moon while the LM landed on the surface of the Moon. The LM would then rejoin the CSM and return to Earth. Although the plan was complex, the use of two separate vehicles avoided the need to land the heavy CSM on the Moon and launch it back into space again, which saved a considerable amount of fuel.

The Apollo program went smoothly until January 1967, when a fire broke out in a spacecraft cabin during testing and claimed the lives of astronauts Virgil Grissom, Ed White, and Roger Chaffee. This incident delayed the program briefly while experts redesigned parts of the Apollo spacecraft. The setback, however, was followed in November 1967 by the successful test launch of the Saturn V rocket. Several piloted Apollo missions followed in 1968, including *Apollo 8*, which became the first piloted spacecraft to orbit the Moon. Two more lunar orbital flights followed in early 1969, and by the summer of that year NASA was ready to attempt the first piloted Moon landing.

Men on the Moon. On July 16, 1969, *Apollo 11* lifted off from Cape Canaveral, Florida, on a 250,000-mile (402,250-km) journey to the Moon. The trip took three days. Astronauts Neil Armstrong and Edwin "Buzz" Aldrin then transferred from the CSM to the LM (nicknamed the *Eagle*) and descended to the Moon's surface.

The LM touched down on an area of the Moon called the Sea of Tranquility on July 20, and Armstrong sent the historic message, "Houston, Tranquility Base here. The *Eagle* has landed." A few hours later, Armstrong stepped out of the LM and became the first person to set foot on the Moon, speaking the now-famous words, "That's one small step for [a] man, one giant leap for mankind."

Aldrin joined Armstrong shortly after, and the astronauts explored the Moon's surface for more than two hours, collecting rock and soil samples. The next day they blasted off the Moon's surface and reunited with Michael Collins, who was piloting the CSM. Returning to Earth on July 24, the astronauts were welcomed as heroes.

Apollo 11 was the first of seven U.S. piloted Moon missions between 1969 and 1972. All were fairly routine except for *Apollo 13*, which suffered a small explosion on the way to the Moon. The explosion cut electrical power to the CSM, shutting off its life-support systems and forcing the crew to transfer to the LM. The crew managed to rig up makeshift systems in order to keep the craft operating properly, and *Apollo 13* returned safely to Earth. Later Apollo missions featured the use of a solar-powered lunar rover, or "Moon buggy," that allowed more extensive exploration of the Moon's surface.

Skylab and the Space Shuttle. In May 1973, NASA launched *Skylab,* the first U.S. space station. Made from a Saturn V rocket stage, *Skylab* had an **air lock,** a docking port, and a telescope. Damage that occurred during launch was repaired by the first of three teams of astronauts to visit the station. The astronauts conducted several scientific and medical experiments, and the final crew spent a then-record 84 days in space.

The major U.S. space effort after the Apollo missions was the development of a space vehicle that could land on an airstrip and be used over and over again. Called the space shuttle, the vehicle is launched into orbit like other spacecraft but lands like a plane.

The space shuttle program was approved in 1972, with approach-and-landing test flights starting five years later. On April 12, 1981, the shuttle *Columbia* began a successful 54-hour orbital flight that marked a new era in space exploration. Since that first flight, space shuttles have flown many missions to conduct experiments, launch and repair satellites, and undertake military missions. Each shuttle can carry a crew of up to eight, and the craft can remain in orbit for ten days.

Four other space shuttles—*Challenger, Discovery, Atlantis,* and *Endeavour*—have been built. *Challenger* was involved in the worst accident in the history of space exploration. It broke up just minutes after launching on January 28, 1986, killing the six astronauts aboard and a science teacher invited to participate in the mission. After an investigation identified the cause of the accident, the shuttle was redesigned and flights resumed two years later.

air lock *airtight chamber used to enter and exit a vehicle in space*

Space Probes. Crewed space flights have received the most attention. However, a number of great successes in the U.S. space program have come from unpiloted probes that studied and photographed the Moon and planets of our solar system.

The first U.S. space probes, like those of the Soviet Union, were lunar probes. After several early failures, three Ranger probes reached the Moon in 1965 and took thousands of photographs. The next year, *Surveyor 1* landed on the lunar surface, sending back more than 11,000 pictures before losing power. Between 1966 and 1968 several more Surveyors landed and conducted experiments on the Moon's surface. During the same time, a series of Lunar Orbiters took photos and measured the Moon's gravity, information that was used in choosing landing spots for the Apollo missions.

The first U.S. probe to reach Venus, *Mariner 2,* flew past the planet in 1962 and transmitted measurements and other data to Earth. It was followed by *Mariner 5* in 1967. Seven years later *Mariner 10* sent back images of Venus and then traveled to Mercury. In 1978 *Pioneer Venus 1* and *Pioneer Venus 2* orbited the planet and sent small scientific probes into its atmosphere. In 1990 the probe *Magellan* reached Venus and used radar to penetrate the planet's cloud cover and map its surface.

Between 1965 and 1971 four Mariner probes flew past Mars, photographing the planet and its moons and analyzing the Martian atmosphere. The *Viking 1* and *Viking 2* probes landed on the surface of Mars less than six weeks apart in 1976, and they continued sending data to Earth until 1982. In 1997 the *Mars Pathfinder* probe also landed on and sent data from Mars.

The United States has been alone in exploring the outer solar system. In 1973 the probe *Pioneer 10* reached Jupiter and analyzed the planet's atmosphere. *Pioneer 11,* launched in 1973, also flew by Jupiter and was later sent to explore Saturn. *Voyager 1* and *Voyager 2* provided the most important data, as well as incredible photographs, of both Jupiter and Saturn between 1979 and 1981. *Voyager 2* continued on to Uranus in 1986 and Neptune in 1989, discovering rings around both planets and studying the planets and their moons. *Galileo,* launched in 1989, took close-up images of the asteroids that lie between the orbits of Mars and Jupiter and sent an instrumented probe into Jupiter's atmosphere.

Recent Efforts at Space Exploration

The collapse of the Soviet Union in the early 1990s brought an end to the 40-year space race between that nation and the United States. Meanwhile, a number of other nations have entered the field of space exploration, making it a truly international undertaking.

By the mid-1960s European nations had begun designing rockets and satellites. In 1975, 14 Western European nations joined to form the European Space Agency (ESA), combining their resources to develop spacecraft and equipment. ESA oversaw the building of Spacelab, a scientific laboratory that has flown aboard the space shuttle. ESA has also launched probes to study the Sun and Halley's comet, as well as commercial satellites. Since 1970 a number of other countries have also launched satellites for commercial and scientific purposes, including Japan, China, India, Israel, Italy, Brazil, Sweden, South Africa, and several Arab nations.

The focus in space exploration today is on cooperation rather than competition. The United States and several other nations have been working together to develop the *International Space Station*, to be crewed by astronauts from all over the world. The United States and other nations are also researching and developing new rockets, space vehicles, and other space technologies.

Longer-range plans include the possibility of establishing bases on the Moon or Mars that might one day be used to gather mineral resources and serve as launching areas for further space exploration. By working together and combining the knowledge and skills of researchers, scientists, and technicians from all over the world, humans may be on the brink of a new era in space exploration. *See also* Apollo Program; Armstrong, Neil; Astronauts; Cape Canaveral; Challenger Disaster; Cosmonauts; European Space Agency; Gagarin, Yuri; Goddard, Robert; Korolev, Sergei; Leonov, Alexei; Mars Probes; Mir; Moon; NASA; Oberth, Hermann; Ride, Sally; Rockets; Salyut Space Stations; Satellites; Shepard, Alan; Skylab; Soyuz Spacecraft; Spacecraft, Parts of; Space Probes; Space Rovers; Space Shuttles; Space Stations; Space Suits; Space Travel; Space Walks; Sputnik 1; Tereshkova, Valentina; Tsiolkovsky, Konstantin; Viking Space Probes; Voyager Space Probes.

Space Probes

A space probe is an unpiloted spacecraft used to explore and collect scientific information in space. Probes provide scientists with information about the solar system that cannot be gathered from Earth, and they do so at far less cost and risk than human space missions.

Probes have photographed and made scientific measurements of comets, asteroids, the Sun, and every planet in the solar system except Pluto. Probes have landed on Venus and Mars, our nearest planetary neighbors, and they paved the way for the Apollo missions that sent astronauts to the Moon.

History of Space Probes

Early space probes were used to study the Moon, Mars, and Venus. Later probes headed for more distant targets, including the Sun and the outer planets.

lunar referring to the Moon

Moon Probes. In 1959 the Soviet Union's *Luna 1* probe passed less than 4,000 miles (6,440 km) from the Moon and the *Luna 2* probe actually hit the Moon at high speed. U.S. Ranger probes took close-up pictures of the **lunar** surface in 1964 and 1965. The following year the Soviet *Luna 9* capsule was ejected onto the surface of the Moon, and the U.S. *Surveyor 1* probe completed a soft landing—a gentle approach to the surface. The U.S. Lunar Orbiters, five probes that circled the Moon in 1966 and 1967, sent back photographs that were used to select a landing site for the Apollo missions. The orbiters also detected irregularities in the Moon's gravity, information that proved critical for planning safe lunar landings.

Mars Probes. The first probe to photograph and gather data about Mars, the U.S. *Mariner 4,* was launched in 1964. *Mariner 9,* which orbited Mars in 1971, photographed the entire surface of the planet as well as its two moons.

Two U.S. Viking probes landed on Mars in 1976 and transmitted data to Earth for years. The U.S. *Mars Pathfinder,* which landed on Mars in 1997, sent back stunning color photographs and confirmed that Mars was once covered with water. The *Mars Polar Lander,* launched in 1999, was designed to search for water near the planet's south pole.

Venus Probes. In 1962 the U.S. *Mariner 2* became the first probe to relay data from Venus. *Mariner 5* studied the planet in 1967, and seven years later, *Mariner 10* transmitted images from Venus and then traveled to Mercury. By 1975 several Soviet Venera probes had reached the surface and transmitted information for nearly two hours before being destroyed by the intense heat and pressure of the planet's atmosphere. In 1983 *Venera 15* and *Venera 16* used radar to map the north polar region of Venus. Seven years later the U.S. *Magellan* craft mapped the entire surface and produced detailed images of the planet's craters, plains, and ridges.

Probes to the Outer Solar System. The United States has launched the only successful missions to explore the planets beyond Mars. *Pioneer 10* visited Jupiter in 1973, and *Pioneer 11* reached Saturn in 1979. They were followed by the Voyager probes, which returned more data on both planets. In 1986 and 1989, *Voyager 2* flew past Uranus and Neptune, taking photos of the planets, their rings, and their moons. In 1994 the *Galileo* space probe witnessed the collision of comet Shoemaker-Levy 9 with Jupiter.

Prospecting in Space

Space probes offer exciting opportunities for obtaining natural resources from space. Scientists believe that both water and rare minerals may be found elsewhere in the solar system. In the United States a group of researchers is organizing a privately funded mission to send a space probe to one of the asteroids that pass close to Earth. The probe will release landing devices containing instruments to study the composition of the rocky asteroid. If the visit uncovers valuable resources—such as minerals that are becoming scarce on Earth—future missions could include mining the asteroid to extract its wealth.

The mission of the Cassini space probe includes close approaches to Venus and Jupiter, followed by an extended exploration of Saturn. The probe is scheduled to continue observing Saturn and its moons until about 2008.

Other Probes. Since 1965 the Sun has been studied by a number of probes, including *Ulysses,* which was launched by the United States for the European Space Agency in 1990. The first probe to examine a comet at close range was **NASA**'s *International Cometary Explorer,* which passed the comet Giacobini-Zinner in 1985. The following year the first European interplanetary probe, *Giotto,* passed close to the core of Halley's comet. In 1999 the U.S. launched *Stardust,* a probe built to collect dust and particles from comets and other objects in space for study on Earth.

Parts and Operation

Space probes are complicated pieces of equipment designed to operate for years in the hostile environment of space. In addition to scientific instruments, they carry equipment to provide power, **propulsion,** communications, and internal monitoring.

Power and Guidance. Space probes must supply their own power to run all the equipment on board. Those that operate near the Sun often use solar panels to collect energy from the Sun and convert it to electricity. Those traveling far from the Sun use nuclear power units.

Space probes must be able to stay on course across millions of miles of space to reach their destinations. They are guided by onboard computers and remote control signals transmitted from a ground station. Small rockets attached to the probe may be fired in order to change its course. Orbiters, probes designed to circle a planet, usually have a larger rocket to slow them down and place them in orbit.

Other navigation devices help position the probe so that equipment such as cameras and radio transmitters face in the proper direction. Some probes are set spinning during launch or shortly thereafter. This motion acts like a **gyroscope** to stabilize the probe. Small jets or electrically powered wheels spinning inside the craft may be used to rotate it. Sun **sensors** and star scanners keep probes on course by tracking fixed points of reference in space. This is especially important for probes operating in distant regions, where radio commands from Earth may take hours to arrive.

Communications. Because a probe's primary mission is to gather information and transmit it to Earth, its communications equipment is extremely important. Transmitters and an antenna send a constant stream of information, called telemetry. In addition to scientific data, the probe reports on the functioning of its own systems. Radio equipment on board also receives commands sent from a ground station on Earth. NASA's Deep Space Network includes ground stations in the United States, Spain, and Australia that communicate with probes and other spacecraft.

Command System. Every probe has a main computer that controls and coordinates the operation of the other systems. The command system stores instructions sent from Earth and carries them out on

NASA *National Aeronautics and Space Administration, the U.S. space agency*

propulsion *process of driving or propelling*

gyroscope *spinning mechanism that maintains its position even when the framework supporting it is tilted*

sensor *device that reacts to changes in light, heat, motion, and so on*

schedule. It also stores data gathered by instruments and codes it for telemetry. The command system detects any failures or problems that could affect the functioning of the probe. It can shut down systems to prevent damage and restart them when the problem has been solved.

See also EUROPEAN SPACE AGENCY; MARS PROBES; MOON; NASA; SATELLITES; SPACECRAFT, PARTS OF; SPACE EXPLORATION; SPACE ROVERS; VIKING SPACE PROBES; VOYAGER SPACE PROBES.

Space Rovers

Soviet Union nation that existed from 1922 to 1991, made up of Russia and 14 other republics in eastern Europe and northern Asia

extraterrestrial from or located outside the Earth or its atmosphere

probe uncrewed spacecraft sent out to explore and collect information in space

lunar referring to the Moon

vacuum empty space with low air pressure

A space rover is a wheeled vehicle designed to travel on the surface of another planet or a moon. Both the **Soviet Union** and the United States have used such vehicles for **extraterrestrial** exploration.

Lunokhod 1, which traveled to the Moon aboard the Soviet **probe** *Luna 17* in 1970, was the first roving vehicle used on a mission. The vehicle photographed the Moon and drilled into its surface to collect rock and soil samples. *Lunokhod 2* was sent to the Moon in 1973 to conduct further research. The missions demonstrated that it was possible to explore extraterrestrial regions with remote-controlled vehicles.

The United States used a space vehicle during the last three Apollo missions in 1971 and 1972. The **lunar** roving vehicle (LRV) was a passenger vehicle with enough room for two people and scientific equipment. Light and tough, the rover traveled at a speed of about 7 miles (11 km) per hour and could cover a total distance of about 55 miles (88 km) on its electric power supply. It had wire mesh wheels because air-filled tires would explode in the **vacuum** of the Moon's atmosphere. The rover's computerized navigation system helped the astronauts keep track of their location. On each of its missions, the LRV transported hundreds of pounds of lunar rocks.

This six-wheeled roving vehicle was designed to explore the surface of Mars.

Sojourner, a robotic space vehicle, landed on Mars with the U.S. probe *Mars Pathfinder* in July 1997. It carried color cameras to send back pictures of the Martian surface, as well as instruments for studying the planet's rocks, soil, and dust. *Sojourner* transmitted thousands of photographs to Earth before the mission ended in November 1997. *See also* APOLLO PROGRAM; MARS PROBES; NASA; SPACE EXPLORATION; SPACE PROBES.

Space Shuttles

NASA *National Aeronautics and Space Administration, the U.S. space agency*

A space shuttle is a reusable spacecraft designed to carry a crew and cargo into orbit and then to return to Earth and land like an airplane. Since the first orbital flight of the U.S. space shuttle *Columbia* in 1981, **NASA** has been launching an average of four to five shuttles a year. The missions have included such activities as launching, retrieving, and repairing satellites; conducting scientific experiments; and performing secret military tasks. The space shuttles are also playing an important role in the construction and operation of the *International Space Station* orbiting the Earth.

History of Space Shuttles

In the 1930s scientists in Germany began working on plans for a reusable spacecraft. However, German leaders were more interested in developing a rocket-missile program. In any case, the outbreak of World War II halted such projects.

Early Rocket Planes. Engineers in the 1950s and 1960s were eager to build planes that could go faster and higher than ever before. One program in the United States led to the development of the X-15 rocket plane. Instead of taking off from a runway, the X-15 was carried into the air beneath the wings of a B-52 bomber and then released.

Between 1959 and 1968, X-15s flew more than 100 missions and broke many speed records. The planes reached a record altitude of 67 miles (108 km), demonstrating that a rocket-powered craft could fly into space, return to Earth, and land safely on a runway. The X-15 also proved that a well-designed rocket plane could function at high altitudes. Earlier craft often spun out of control because the atmosphere was too thin for their rudders, **ailerons,** and flaps to operate properly. The X-15 had large fins that helped stabilize the craft, and it used small jets—like those on U.S. spacecraft of the time—to steer the plane at high altitudes.

aileron *movable section on aircraft wing, used to turn the plane*

The Space Shuttle Program. In 1972 President Richard Nixon approved the development of the Space Transportation System (STS), a program recommended by a commission a few years earlier. The STS later became known as the space shuttle.

The first flights of the STS program began in 1977 with the test vehicle *Enterprise.* The *Enterprise* was carried by a Boeing 747 airliner to an altitude of 22,000 feet (6,700 m) and released so that pilots could test its

The space shuttle Columbia was first launched into orbit on April 12, 1981. That successful test flight began the era of space shuttle missions.

aerodynamics *branch of science that deals with the motion of air and the effects of such motion on planes and other objects*

payload *object placed in space by a launch vehicle; any type of cargo carried aboard a spacecraft*

aerodynamics as well as its gliding and landing ability. In April 1981, NASA launched the shuttle *Columbia* into space with a crew of two astronauts for the first of four orbital test flights.

Early shuttle flights showed that the spacecraft was reliable. The crew size soon expanded from two to four astronauts, and later, to seven or eight. Current shuttle crews include not only pilots, but also mission specialists—experts on shuttle operations—and **payload** specialists—experts who conduct scientific research aboard the shuttle.

Between 1981 and 1986 the U.S. space shuttle fleet expanded to include four vehicles: *Columbia, Challenger, Discovery,* and *Atlantis.* Twenty-four missions were successfully completed during this period. NASA began to consider the possibility of inviting scientists and ordinary American citizens to participate in shuttle missions, and in 1984 it introduced a "Space Flight Participation Program." The first citizen chosen under this program was Christa McAuliffe, a schoolteacher from New Hampshire.

The Challenger Disaster.   On January 28, 1986, the space shuttle *Challenger* lifted off from Cape Canaveral, Florida, carrying McAuliffe and six astronauts. Just 73 seconds after launch, the shuttle broke apart and exploded, killing all seven people aboard.

An investigation into the *Challenger* disaster revealed that problems with seals, called O-rings, on the shuttle's solid rocket boosters had caused the accident. The investigation also revealed that NASA officials had proceeded with the launch despite the fact that engineers had warned that the cool temperatures on the day of the launch might lead to problems.

The *Challenger* tragedy shut down the U.S. space shuttle program for 32 months while the launch rockets were redesigned and new safety procedures were put in place. The program resumed in September 1988, with the launch of the shuttle *Discovery*. A new vehicle, *Endeavour*, was built to replace *Challenger*. Since the program resumed, the space shuttles have performed many missions without incident.

Shuttle Operations

Space shuttles are very complicated vehicles designed to be reused for at least 100 separate missions. They have become an indispensable part of the U.S. space program and are considered a vital step toward the future of space exploration and travel.

Parts of the Shuttle. The space shuttle consists of three basic parts: the orbiter, which carries crew and cargo; an external fuel tank that contains liquid fuel for the orbiter's engines; and two solid-fuel rocket boosters. The rocket boosters and external fuel tank are used only during the launching.

At launch, the boosters and the orbiter's main engines fire, and the shuttle lifts off from the launchpad. After about two minutes, the boosters run out of fuel and are ejected from the shuttle. Parachutes on the boosters slow their descent to the ocean, where they are recovered for reuse on later missions.

After feeding fuel to the orbiter—generally for a period of about eight minutes—the external tank is discarded and burns up during reentry into Earth's atmosphere. The orbiter's main engines continue to lift the shuttle into orbit. These engines are used again at the end of the mission to slow the orbiter as it prepares to return to Earth.

The most important part of the shuttle system is the orbiter, which measures 184 feet (56 m) in length and has a wingspan of 78 feet (24 m). Resembling a conventional airplane to some extent, the orbiter contains a two-level cabin with a cockpit and workstation in the upper level and living quarters and storage areas in the lower level. The lower level includes space for conducting small experiments and an **air lock** that leads into the cargo area, or payload bay.

The payload bay, located in the center of the orbiter, is 60 feet (18 m) long and 15 feet (4.6 m) across—large enough to carry two or more satellites. Two large doors on the payload bay open to allow scientific instruments to be exposed to space, to enable astronauts to work outside the shuttle, and to release excess heat into space to keep the shuttle from overheating. At the edge of the payload bay is a large robotic arm—the Remote Manipulator System (RMS)—that astronauts can use to **maneuver** satellites.

The tail section of the orbiter contains the shuttle's main rocket engines. Smaller rockets used to maneuver the orbiter in space are also in the tail section.

The Fernbomber

Long before most people considered spaceflight a serious possibility, German scientists Eugene Sanger and Irene Bredt developed plans in 1937 for a reusable spacecraft. Called the Fernbomber (long-range bomber), their proposed craft would have the ability to bomb cities 12,000 miles (19,300 km) away. But the German government never followed through on the project, deciding instead to devote its energies to research that led to the development of the first long-range guided missile, the V-2 rocket.

air lock airtight chamber used to enter and exit a vehicle in space

maneuver to make a series of changes in course

Covering the orbiter is a collection of more than 25,000 ceramic-coated tiles. These tiles, made of special silica fiber, can endure the tremendous heat encountered during reentry into the atmosphere. Although the tiles reach temperatures up to 3,000°F (1,650°C), they can be handled safely just minutes after the shuttle lands.

Shuttle Missions. The space shuttles are designed to remain in space up to 14 days, usually at an altitude of between 150 and 200 miles (240 to 320 km) above the Earth. Launches and most landings take place at the Kennedy Space Center in Florida; however, bad weather there sometimes shifts landings to Edwards Air Force Base in California.

The majority of shuttle missions involve satellite operations or scientific experiments. Military missions, common in the 1980s, were discontinued in the early 1990s. Satellite operations include the launching, repair, and retrieval of communications, weather, and other types of satellites. Shuttles have also been used to launch space probes and orbiting scientific instruments, such as the Hubble Space Telescope and the Gamma Ray Observatory.

Scientific missions aboard the shuttle include experiments to test the effects of weightlessness on materials and manufacturing processes, as well as medical studies in space. The most extensive experiments are conducted using Spacelab, a self-contained scientific laboratory developed by the European Space Agency (ESA). Spacelab fits into the orbiter's payload bay and is connected to the crew cabin by a tunnel.

NASA is using the space shuttles to carry parts, equipment, and workers into orbit to assemble the *International Space Station,* scheduled for completion in about 2004. The experience gained by conducting experiments aboard the shuttle, and by working on satellites outside the orbiter, will be valuable in building the space station, as well as in preparing humans for extended space missions to Mars or other planets in the solar system. *See also* CHALLENGER DISASTER; EUROPEAN SPACE AGENCY; NASA; SPACE EXPLORATION; SPACE STATIONS; SPACE TRAVEL; TELESCOPES.

The Soviet Shuttle

In the 1980s the Soviet Union developed its own space shuttle. Called *Buran,* meaning "snowstorm," it resembled the U.S. space shuttles in many ways. An unpiloted version of *Buran* was launched on November 15, 1988. It flew twice around the Earth and landed safely in a region of the Soviet Union called Kazakhstan. Though a second shuttle was built, no further flights were made because the program ran out of funds.

Space Stations

probe *uncrewed spacecraft sent out to explore and collect information in space*

Soviet Union *nation that existed from 1922 to 1991, made up of Russia and 14 other republics in eastern Europe and northern Asia*

A space station is a structure made by humans that orbits the Earth. Designed to be occupied by people for extended periods, space stations can serve as places to conduct scientific experiments or launch satellites or space **probes,** or they can be used as stopping-off points for piloted missions to the Moon or other planets.

Starting in the early 1970s, both the United States and the former **Soviet Union** launched space stations. The Russian *Mir* achieved an endurance record, remaining in orbit for more than 13 years. In the late 1990s, several nations combined forces to begin construction of the very large and elaborate *International Space Station.*

History of Space Stations

One of the first people to envision a space station orbiting the Earth was Russian scientist Konstantin Tsiolkovsky. In the late 1800s he wrote about how it would be possible to build a large, cylinder-shaped craft that would spin to create artificial gravity. Green plants growing aboard the spacecraft would provide both food and oxygen for the crew. In the mid-1900s other scientists, such as the German rocket pioneer Wernher von Braun, proposed similar ideas.

Salyut. In April 1971, the Soviet Union launched *Salyut 1,* the first operational space station. Three **cosmonauts** lived aboard the station for three weeks in June 1971, but an accident claimed their lives as they returned to Earth in the spacecraft *Soyuz 11.* Despite that tragedy, *Salyut 1* did prove that humans could spend long periods in space.

Salyut 1 fell out of orbit after six months and burned up in Earth's atmosphere. Six other Salyut stations were launched between 1973 and 1982, with the final two being particularly successful. *Salyut 6* and *Salyut 7* had the ability to receive robot-controlled supply ships carrying additional food and fuel, allowing the crews to stay on board for months at a time.

Salyut crews conducted many scientific experiments and gave cosmonauts valuable experience in working outside the station and dealing with the effects of long-term weightlessness. Last occupied in March 1986, *Salyut 7* fell back to Earth in 1991.

Skylab. The first and only U.S. space station was *Skylab,* launched in May 1973. *Skylab* was constructed from part of a Saturn V rocket, the same type of rocket used to launch Apollo missions to the Moon. The station—more than twice as long and almost twice as wide as the Salyut stations—provided comfortable quarters for the three-member crews that served aboard it.

Like Salyut, *Skylab* had a difficult start. Several of its parts were damaged during launch, and the first astronauts to visit the station had to repair a jammed solar panel and replace a thermal (heat) shield that had been torn away. Although these repairs required a good deal of work outside the station, the crew completed the job successfully and spent a record 28 days in space.

Two more missions to *Skylab* took place in 1973. The final one included a space walk of more than 7 hours—the longest up to that time—as well as a record 22 hours spent working outside the vehicle on a single mission. The mission also set an endurance record of 84 days in orbit.

Skylab missions produced vital information about the physical and psychological effects on humans of extended stays in space. They also provided astronauts with valuable experience making repairs and performing maintenance on a space station. NASA—the National Aeronautics and Space Administration—had hoped to fly its planned space shuttle to *Skylab.* But the station fell out of orbit in 1979, two years before the first U.S. space shuttle was launched.

Mir. The Soviet Union followed its Salyut program with a new space station called *Mir,* launched in February 1986. *Mir* was designed as a modular station, which meant that it could be expanded by adding extra sections, or modules. The core module contained crew quarters, docking

---

cosmonaut *Russian term for a person who travels into space; literally, "traveler to the universe"*

Escaping Gravity's Pull

Scientists on the *International Space Station* will probably study the effects of weightlessness on the production of certain materials. For example, fiber-optic cables—which contain thin strands of glass that transmit signals—play a vital role in modern communications. When manufactured on Earth, fiber-optic strands contain flaws caused by the pull of gravity. These imperfections reduce their ability to transmit data. However, strands made in the weightless environment of space without gravity's pull would be free of flaws. Weightlessness also provides a good environment for growing almost flawless crystals for use in superfast computer chips.

A member of the crew of the space shuttle Endeavour helped set up a module of the International Space Station in December 1998.

propulsion *process of driving or propelling*

ports where spacecraft could connect to the station, and a power and **propulsion** unit. Other modules designed for technological and scientific research were launched and attached to the core module later. One of them contained hatches for a space shuttle called *Buran* that the Soviets were developing.

Missions to *Mir* featured many scientific experiments, and the crews that stayed at the station set a number of records for time spent in space. In 1987 cosmonaut Yuri Romanenko spent a record 326 days aboard *Mir* and showed no ill effects on his return to Earth, proving that extended stays in space were possible. *Mir* accommodated crews until late 1998. During the 1990s, a number of American astronauts worked with the Russian cosmonauts on the space station.

International Space Station

After *Skylab,* space engineers in the United States began working on similar projects. In 1984 President Ronald Reagan approved plans for building a large space station called *Freedom,* scheduled for completion by the mid-1990s.

Within a few years the European Space Agency, Japan, and Canada had agreed to provide components for the new space station. But as costs kept rising and work fell behind schedule, it appeared that the station might never become a reality.

International Cooperation.

The collapse of the Soviet Union in 1991 provided an opportunity to bring Russia into this international space station as a partner. The aim was to relieve the United States of some of the burden for the project and also to provide work for Russian scientists who might otherwise assist on military projects with countries unfriendly to the United States. Canada, Japan, Italy, Brazil, and the European Space Agency (ESA) are also partners in developing and launching what will be the largest and most complex space station ever.

Scheduled for completion in 2004, the *International Space Station* will represent a major step forward in space exploration and science. Knowledge gained there might solve many problems related to long piloted space flights, such as a mission to Mars. Scientific research in weightless conditions could lead to breakthroughs in medicine, manufacturing, and various sciences. The station also represents an opportunity for nations to use space as an area for peaceful cooperation instead of competition.

Design and Construction.

Known simply as the *International Space Station*, the proposed structure will be the largest human-made object in space—more than 350 feet (107 m) long with 46,000 cubic feet (1,288 cu m) of living and working space. Some 27,000 square feet (2,511 sq m) of solar panels will use energy from the Sun to generate electrical power.

The crew of the station will be housed in a module more than 26 feet (8 m) long. This area will contain a kitchen, a medical area, and an exercise space with stationary bicycles and other equipment designed to strengthen muscle tissue, which deteriorates during long periods of weightlessness. There will be no specific sleeping areas. Instead, crew members will use sleeping bags attached to the walls. Additional modules of the station will include scientific laboratories, docking ports, and a robotic arm for releasing **payloads** and repairing artificial satellites.

payload object placed in space by a launch vehicle; any type of cargo carried aboard a spacecraft

The space station must have enough power, water, and oxygen to support a crew for extended periods. The station's solar panels will provide power, and unused electricity will be stored in batteries. Supplying air and water will be more difficult because of the large amounts required. Moisture released by sweating and breathing may be collected, purified, and recycled for drinking. Another system might recycle and reuse water used for showering and washing. A constant supply of oxygen could be obtained by recycling and converting, through a special process, the carbon dioxide exhaled by the crew.

The various modules of the space station will be built on Earth but launched separately into orbit and then assembled in space. About 40 flights will probably be necessary to carry all the modules and supplies into space. After years of planning and construction, the first sections of the *International Space Station* were finally sent into orbit in late 1998. In May of the following year, astronauts aboard the space shuttle

Discovery docked with the station and then spent six days loading it with supplies and equipment. *See also* EUROPEAN SPACE AGENCY; MIR; NASA; SALYUT SPACE STATIONS; SKYLAB; SPACECRAFT, PARTS OF; SPACE EXPLORATION; SPACE ROVERS; SPACE SHUTTLES; SPACE SUITS; SPACE TRAVEL; SPACE WALKS; TSIOLKOVSKY, KONSTANTIN.

Space Suits

atmospheric pressure *pressure exerted by the Earth's atmosphere at any given point on the planet's surface*

NASA *National Aeronautics and Space Administration, the U.S. space agency*

mobility *ability to move about*

maneuver *series of changes in course*

Astronaut Story Musgrave tests his space suit during preparation for a space shuttle mission.

Space is hostile to human life. It lacks the oxygen and **atmospheric pressure** living beings need. Temperatures may reach 250°F (121°C) in sunlight and drop to –250°F (–121°C) in shadow. Particles called micrometeoroids zip past at up to 60 miles per second (97 km per second). Space suits provide protection from these deadly conditions for people traveling beyond the Earth's atmosphere.

Early Space Suits. Some features of modern space suits come from outfits designed for deep-sea and high-altitude explorers. In the early 1900s ocean divers used suits that supplied oxygen and controlled air pressure. Airplane pilots of the 1930s wore diving suits modified for high-altitude flight.

By the early 1960s jet pilot outfits had been adapted for **NASA**'s Mercury missions. Made of nylon coated with rubber and aluminum, the Mercury space suits could provide air pressure and oxygen if needed. However, crew members had trouble bending their arms and legs when the garments were inflated.

Between 1965 and 1972, several Gemini and Apollo missions included extravehicular activities (EVAs)—tasks in which astronauts left their spacecraft. Designers developed space suits that would protect crew members in deep space and give them greater **mobility** to carry out complex **maneuvers.** The Apollo suits had to be flexible enough to allow the astronauts to ride in the lunar rover, collect rock samples, and conduct experiments. These suits included molded rubber joints at the shoulders, elbows, hips, and knees as well as a backpack with portable life support systems to provide oxygen and air pressure.

Advancing Technology. Astronauts on space shuttle and space station missions use two types of space suits. They wear partial-pressure suits inside the spacecraft while leaving and reentering the Earth's atmosphere. These suits are equipped with communications links and parachute packs in case crew members need to exit from the vehicle in an emergency.

For EVAs the astronauts wear an extravehicular mobility unit (EMU), the most flexible space suit yet developed. It consists of a series of parts and layers. The first layer includes a urine-collection device and a one-piece mesh suit with cooling tubes to protect the astronauts from overheating. Next, crew members put on a drink bag containing water, a cap with headphones and microphones, and a set of instruments that monitor their physical condition.

Astronauts then climb into the two-part outer suit, made of several layers of protective fabric. The primary life support system, which maintains temperature and air circulation, is attached to the hard shell upper section. Tubes between the two halves of the suit allow water and gas to circulate freely. Finally, the astronauts don gloves and a helmet with lights. The complete space suit assembly weighs about 100 pounds (45 kg).

For activities such as repairing spacecraft and retrieving equipment, astronauts also wear a manned maneuvering unit (MMU), a backpack unit loaded with high-pressure nitrogen gas. Operated by hand controls, the MMU releases the gas to propel the astronaut through space—the ultimate in personal transportation. *See also* ASTRONAUTS; ATMOSPHERIC PRESSURE; COSMONAUTS; MOON; SPACE EXPLORATION; SPACE TRAVEL; SPACE WALKS.

Space Travel

Soviet Union *nation that existed from 1922 to 1991, made up of Russia and 14 other republics in eastern Europe and northern Asia*

cosmonaut *Russian term for a person who travels into space; literally, "traveler to the universe"*

Further Information
To learn more about space travel, including the people who have traveled into space and the vehicles and equipment used by them, see the related articles listed at the end of this entry.

Escaping the bounds of Earth to explore the reaches of space is one of the great achievements of modern science. When the **Soviet Union** launched *Sputnik 1,* the first artificial satellite, in 1957, no one knew much about the effects of space travel on machines—let alone on human beings. Yet within a few decades American astronauts had landed and walked on the Moon, and Soviet **cosmonauts** had spent extended periods living and working aboard orbiting space stations.

Launch, Flight, and Return

The basic challenges of space flight are launching a vehicle into space, maintaining control of it, and bringing it safely home at the end of its mission.

Launching. The first great obstacle to space flight was developing enough speed to leave the Earth's atmosphere. A vehicle must travel about 17,500 miles per hour (28,160 km per hour) to achieve orbital velocity—the speed needed to enter orbit around Earth and resist being pulled back to the ground by gravity. To leave orbit and travel away from the Earth, a spacecraft must reach escape velocity, which is 25,000 miles per hour (40,225 km per hour). To arrive at such speeds, spacecraft must be propelled by powerful rockets that burn enormous amounts of fuel. As a result, most of a launch vehicle's weight is taken up by fuel.

Rockets are usually launched in stages, with several rocket units stacked on top of each other. The largest and most powerful rocket is used to launch the vehicle from the ground. When this first-stage rocket has burned all its fuel, it separates from the craft and the second-stage rockets are fired. Most spacecraft also have a third stage and some even have a fourth. As the craft loses its rockets, it becomes lighter. As it goes higher, the pull of gravity decreases. After reaching orbital velocity, the spacecraft levels off to fly parallel with the Earth's surface and circle it. If the craft is programmed to travel farther into space, it keeps accelerating until it breaks free of Earth's gravity completely.

Navigation and Control. Navigation in space can be quite complicated because spacecraft do not move in a straight line toward

The space shuttle broke new ground in many areas of space travel. It was the first reusable space vehicle and the first spacecraft to land like an airplane on its return to Earth.

gyroscope *spinning mechanism that maintains its position even when the framework supporting it is tilted*

vacuum *empty space with low air pressure*

drag *slowing effect of an opposing force, such as friction, on a vehicle*

probe *spacecraft sent out to explore and collect information in space*

maneuver *series of changes in course*

celestial *having to do with the sky or heavens*

their destinations. Moreover, there are few fixed points in space to use as guides to navigation. Before launch, flight engineers calculate the most efficient path, or trajectory, for the spacecraft to take. Internal guidance systems based on **gyroscopes** keep the spacecraft on course.

In the **vacuum** of space there is little friction to create **drag** on a spacecraft. A vehicle will continue moving in the same direction unless another force is applied to it. A spacecraft such as a space **probe** can change its course by firing small thruster rockets. For a satellite orbiting the Earth, little **maneuvering** is necessary. The speed of the orbiting craft balances the pull of gravity and keeps it circling the Earth.

Many piloted space flights involve more complex maneuvers such as rendezvous and docking. Rendezvous occurs when one vehicle passes close by another in space. Docking involves a meeting of and connection between the two vehicles. Both rendezvous and docking are delicate maneuvers that require radar and computers to control the flight path, speed, and position of the two vehicles. U.S. space crews generally assume control of the operation when the two craft are close to each other, but the docking of Russian spacecraft has often been directed by computers.

Spacecraft traveling far out into the solar system and beyond often rely on the gravity of planets to help them along. A spacecraft will accelerate when it enters the gravitational field of a **celestial** body. The vehicle then adjusts its course, and the additional speed acts like a slingshot to hurl the craft toward its destination. Several space probes, such as *Voyager 1, Voyager 2,* and *Galileo,* have used this technique to explore distant planets.

During a mission, a team in the control center tracks the spacecraft and maintains radio and radar contact with it. A worldwide network of tracking stations equipped with large antennae has been established for this purpose. **NASA** has also developed satellite-based tracking **facilities** for monitoring space shuttle flights. Tracking stations receive radio signals—known as telemetry—from the spacecraft that include data such as temperature, pressure, speed, and trajectory. At the same time, the control center may send commands to the spacecraft to turn certain systems on or off, fire rockets to change its course, or check the performance of onboard systems. Most spacecraft systems have several backup systems in case the main system fails.

On a piloted mission the need for communication with mission control is vital. Once in space, a vehicle is far from technical assistance and replacement parts, so if a problem arises, the crew must try to correct it on their own. When an explosion occurred on the *Apollo 13,* the crew survived in the lunar lander by rigging a makeshift device to purify the cabin air. Step-by-step instructions from the mission control team guided the astronauts through the crisis.

Reentry and Recovery. Many spacecraft, such as satellites and space probes, never return to Earth. After a space probe has performed its mission, it keeps drifting into deep space or is abandoned in orbit around or on the surface of the celestial body it is studying. Some satellites remain in orbit after they have stopped functioning, but many reenter Earth's atmosphere, where they burn up. However, all crewed spacecraft are designed to return safely to Earth.

The first challenge of reentry is achieving the proper speed and position when entering the atmosphere. If the spacecraft approaches at too shallow an angle, it will bounce off the Earth's atmosphere like a stone skipping on a pond. If the angle is too steep, the spacecraft will be unable to withstand the sudden increase in the pull of gravity. Heat is another problem in reentry. Air surrounding the rapidly moving vehicle can reach 10,000°F (5,540°C). To survive such temperatures, early spacecraft had heat shields that would absorb the heat and burn away in layers. The ceramic-coated tiles protecting the space shuttle can take the heat directly.

Before the space shuttle, U.S. piloted spacecraft parachuted to a soft landing in the ocean, where they were recovered by a naval ship. Russian spacecraft have used both parachutes and retro-rockets—small rockets fired in the direction opposite to their flight path—to slow them down in order to land on solid ground. The space shuttle was the first spacecraft designed to glide to a landing like an airplane.

Survival in Space

The most urgent questions posed by early space pioneers were whether, and how, humans could withstand the hostile environment of space. Space travelers would need not only food and water but also air to

NASA *National Aeronautics and Space Administration, the U.S. space agency*

facilities *something built or created to serve a particular function*

During training, astronauts practice living in the gravity-free environment of space. They also learn to take steps to protect their bodies from the effects of long-term weightlessness.

radiation energy given off in waves or particles

breathe. They would need protection from intense heat and cold and from **radiation** released by the Sun and other objects in space. They would also need to learn to function in a weightless environment.

Weightlessness. Humans are accustomed to the pull of Earth's gravity, the attraction between the mass of the Earth and the mass of one's body. But the strength of gravity varies throughout the universe. The Moon's gravity is only one-sixth that of the Earth, and on Jupiter gravity is $2\frac{1}{2}$ times stronger than on Earth. In space, objects experience weightlessness, or microgravity, a state in which they feel almost no pull of gravity. People and equipment float freely, and many ordinary activities, such as pouring liquids, require special procedures.

Weightlessness causes various reactions in the human body, including nausea and vomiting. This condition, known as space sickness, usually lasts several days, during which motion sickness medication may be used to relieve it. Weightlessness can also affect an astronaut's sense of direction and balance. After a short time in space, the organs that control balance ignore all directional signals, but they operate normally soon after returning to Earth.

On extended space voyages, the body goes through deconditioning, a process in which the muscles become weak because they do not have to work against the force of gravity. In addition, the heart has a hard time pumping and maintaining blood pressure and the bones begin to lose calcium. Vigorous exercise and a special diet can counter muscle and bone loss. Most of these conditions disappear after a short time back on Earth.

Safety. Every precaution is taken to ensure the safety of space travelers. Powerful acceleration in a spacecraft produces a gravitational pull several times greater than Earth's gravity. This force decreases blood circulation to the brain. Flight engineers have found that they can reduce this effect by placing the astronaut in a reclining position with head slightly raised and knees slightly bent. Spacecraft also contain emergency escape systems in case of failure on the launching pad or while the spacecraft is still in the Earth's atmosphere.

A spacecraft must supply enough fresh air to support its crew during a mission. Crew members breathe a mixture of oxygen and nitrogen that is similar to the Earth's atmosphere. Vehicles are also equipped with systems to remove the carbon dioxide exhaled by crew members, which would otherwise build up and suffocate them. In some spacecraft, fans circulate the cabin air through containers filled with a substance that absorbs carbon dioxide.

When performing tasks outside the spacecraft, astronauts and cosmonauts wear space suits for protection against the harsh environment. The suit contains its own oxygen supply as well as a system to gather and eliminate bodily waste. It is pressurized to counter the vacuum of space and has climate control to maintain a comfortable temperature. Heavy insulation protects the wearer against radiation and harmful particles in space.

Daily Life. Every aspect of life is more challenging aboard a spacecraft. Cramped quarters and weightlessness make eating and drinking a particular challenge. On early space flights, astronauts ate foods contained in plastic pouches. They sucked the food from the pouch through a straw. Today, crew members eat frozen prepared meals that are heated on board. Water, which is carried in storage tanks, is recycled if possible for purposes such as washing. Trash generated during a mission is stowed in storage areas aboard the vehicle or ejected out into space.

Bathing and sleeping in space require some special accommodations. Most astronauts and cosmonauts traveling in spacecraft simply take sponge baths to keep clean. The first space stations were equipped with collapsible showers, but space stations now have permanent shower facilities. To sleep, astronauts can strap their sleeping bags firmly in place or simply float in the air with a few cords connected to the cabin to keep them from bouncing around. *See also* ACCIDENTS; APOLLO PROGRAM; ASTRONAUTS; CAPE CANAVERAL; CHALLENGER DISASTER; COSMONAUTS; GYROSCOPE; MIR; MOON; NASA; ROCKETS; SALYUT SPACE STATIONS; SATELLITES; SKYLAB; SOYUZ SPACECRAFT; SPACECRAFT, PARTS OF; SPACE EXPLORATION; SPACE PROBES; SPACE ROVERS; SPACE SHUTTLES; SPACE SUITS; SPACE WALKS; SPUTNIK 1; VIKING SPACE PROBES; VOYAGER SPACE PROBES.

Verne's Vision

Stories by science fiction writers have sometimes nearly predicted future events. In his 1865 novel *From the Earth to the Moon,* French writer Jules Verne told the tale of men who were launched to the Moon using a giant cannon. Although Verne's fictional method of propulsion bears no resemblance to an actual spacecraft launch, some of his other ideas were remarkably accurate. The craft in his story was launched from southern Florida, the location of the main U.S. launching site, Cape Canaveral. The speed at which his voyagers traveled, 7 miles (11 km) per second, is almost exactly the speed a spacecraft must achieve to break free of Earth's orbit.

A space walk, or extravehicular activity (EVA), occurs when an astronaut or cosmonaut leaves a spacecraft during a mission. Most space walks have involved floating outside a spacecraft that is in orbit around Earth. However, the astronauts who visited the Moon performed EVAs by walking and riding on the Moon's surface.

Early Space Walks. The primary purpose of early space walks was to prove that EVA was possible. The first one took place in March 1965, when Soviet cosmonaut Alexei Leonov stepped from the *Voshkod 2* capsule. Once outside, Leonov found that he could not get back into the spacecraft because the pressure in his space suit made it rigid, and he was unable to bend at the waist. After a moment of panic, Leonov realized that he could release some of the pressure by opening a valve on his space suit. Once he did so, he managed to bend slightly and to pull himself through the hatch.

The first U.S. space walk was completed in June 1965 by Edward H. White II. White spent 21 minutes outside the *Gemini IV* spacecraft while it orbited the Earth at nearly 18,000 miles per hour (29,000 km per hour).

Tasks Performed in Space. Eventually space walks were used to accomplish specific tasks. In 1969 two *Apollo 11* astronauts left the lunar module to raise an American flag, set up scientific equipment, and collect rock and soil samples from the surface of the Moon. In 1973 the U.S. space station *Skylab* lost a solar panel and part of its heat shield during its launch, and another solar panel had jammed. In two space walks, one lasting $3\frac{1}{2}$ hours, the astronauts were able to repair the shield and free the jammed solar panel. Later *Skylab* crews had even longer space walks, and the final crew set records for the longest single EVA (just over 7 hours) and the most total EVA time on a single mission (22 hours and 21 minutes). These efforts demonstrated that humans could work effectively for long periods in space.

In the 1980s and 1990s Russian cosmonauts aboard the *Mir* space station and U.S. astronauts on the space shuttle completed extended EVAs. The Russians made vital repairs to *Mir* during several of their space walks. American shuttle crews have performed EVAs to retrieve and repair satellites in orbit and to conduct scientific experiments.

Equipment. Space walkers wear pressurized suits made of many layers of fabric to protect them from the loss of **atmospheric pressure,** lack of oxygen, extremes of temperature, and **radiation** in deep space. Their backpack unit contains oxygen, water, batteries, and an air treatment system. With this equipment, astronauts can stay outside for up to eight hours.

On most EVAs, astronauts are connected to the spacecraft by a safety line called a tether, which prevents them from floating away. However, on some EVAs, astronauts use the manned maneuvering unit (MMU), a device powered by small compressed nitrogen jets. With the MMU, an astronaut can **maneuver** in space freely and return safely to the spacecraft. *See also* ASTRONAUTS; COSMONAUTS; LEONOV, ALEXEI; MIR; MOON; SKYLAB; SPACE EXPLORATION; SPACE ROVERS; SPACE SHUTTLES; SPACE STATIONS; SPACE SUITS.

atmospheric pressure *pressure exerted by the Earth's atmosphere at any given point on the planet's surface*

radiation *energy given off in waves or particles*

maneuver *to make a series of changes in course*

Spanish Armada

invincible unable to be conquered

maneuver to make a series of changes in course

maritime related to the sea or shipping

In 1588 King Philip II of Spain sent a fleet of warships known as the Armada to invade England. A devout Catholic, King Philip hoped to restore the Roman Catholic faith in Protestant England. He also wanted to put an end to raids by English pirates on Spanish ships and coastal settlements in the Americas. Although hailed by the Spanish as **invincible,** the Armada was swiftly defeated by the English.

In May 1588 the Armada—consisting of about 130 Spanish warships—set out from Lisbon, Portugal. Toward the end of July, it sailed into the English Channel, where it met the English fleet. The Spanish ships were big and well suited to fighting in close formation. But the English ships, though smaller, were fast and easy to **maneuver,** and their guns had a longer range than those on the Spanish vessels. After several unsuccessful encounters with the English fleet, the Spanish decided to anchor in the French port of Calais. The English started fires on eight of their own vessels and sent them drifting into the Armada. Forced to scatter, the big, slow Spanish warships became easy prey for the guns of the English vessels.

The Spanish fleet had been badly battered, but its ordeal was not yet over. Although a favorable wind allowed the Armada to escape by sailing northward around Scotland and Ireland, the fleet was further ravaged by storms in the North Atlantic Ocean. Only about half of the vessels in the Armada, many of them beyond repair, made it back to Spain. Perhaps as many as 15,000 sailors and soldiers perished, many times the English losses.

The defeat of the Spanish Armada not only saved England from invasion, but it also established the nation as a leading **maritime** power. Moreover, the victory opened the way for the country's colonial expansion into North America and India. *See also* SAILBOATS AND SAILING SHIPS.

Spirit of St. Louis

see **Lindbergh, Charles.**

Sports and Recreation

The basic element of all transportation is moving goods and people from one place to another—whether on foot, on horseback, or in a vehicle. Movement plays an important role in sports and recreation as well, and some vehicles used in transportation also appear in competitive and leisure activities.

No Equipment Required. There are many sports and recreational activities for which no special equipment is needed. Walking, the oldest form of transportation, is an inexpensive way for people of all ages to achieve physical fitness and health. Race walking, jogging, and running are all popular among fitness enthusiasts. Competitive running includes various events, ranging from short sprints, or dashes, to long-distance races, including the 26-mile (42-km) marathon.

Hiking usually involves greater distances than walking does. Whether following a trail in the countryside or climbing hills and mountains, people hike to keep physically fit and to enjoy nature. Some hikers make short outings that last a few hours. Others may journey into the wilderness for several days or weeks, carrying backpacks filled with extra clothing, camping gear, and food. Orienteering is a form of competitive hiking in which participants use a map and a compass to arrive at specific points along a route.

Swimming, practiced by the Egyptians as early as 2500 B.C., has never been used as a form of transportation. Among the ancient Greeks and Romans, it developed as a requirement of military training. There is some evidence of competitive swimming in Japan in the 100s B.C., but swimming as a sport did not really begin until the 1800s. Today swimmers can compete in numerous events based on swimming strokes and distance.

Skis, Skates, and More. Some sports and leisure activities call for equipment. Skiing may have developed in Scandinavia as early as 5,000 years ago. For centuries people in the northern and eastern parts of Europe have used skis as a way of traveling over snow. Skiing became a sport in the early 1800s, and today people throughout the world ski for recreation. There are two main types of skiing—downhill and cross-country. In downhill skiing, people descend specially prepared courses on mountain slopes. Cross-country skiing involves traveling along marked or unmarked trails through forests or open terrain. Snowboarding, a variation of skiing, features a single wide board instead of

These cross-country skiers follow a trail through a forest in Lillehammer, Norway.

In-line skating, also called roller-blading, became a popular form of recreation and exercise in the 1980s.

two narrow skis. Waterskiing originated in the 1920s with the development of runners that could be used on water.

Ice skating may have started as early as 1000 B.C. in Scandinavia. By A.D. 500 skating on frozen canals in the winter was popular in Holland. Competitive speed skating originated in Europe in the early 1800s. Figure skating and ice hockey soon followed.

Horseback riding began as a form of transportation, but it has become primarily a sport and recreational activity. Horse racing, enjoyed by ancient Assyrians as early as 3,000 years ago, now attracts fans in many countries. In some places, including ranches in the western United States, people still use horses to get around.

Surfing originated hundreds of years ago as recreation among the Polynesian people on the islands of the Pacific Ocean. Since the early 1960s surfers have competed for world championships on both coasts of North America and in the waters off Australia, Peru, Hawaii, and South Africa.

Skateboarding first appeared in California in the early 1960s. Now skateboards are used for fun, to get around neighborhoods, and in competition with others performing various stunts and turns. In-line skating developed from roller skating, a recreation that became popular after the late 1800s. Unlike roller skates, which have a pair of parallel wheels, in-line skates have a single row of wheels.

Vehicles. Some sports and recreational activities involve vehicles that are also used for transportation. These include sports car racing, sailing and boating, and bicycling. Sailboats, motorboats, canoes, and kayaks can compete in races and can be enjoyed for recreation. Bicycles are an important means of everyday travel in countries such as China, India, and the Netherlands. These two-wheeled, pedal-powered vehicles are also used for racing and recreation in many parts of the world. *See also* BICYCLES; CANOES AND KAYAKS; HORSES; MOTORBOATS; RACE CARS; RECREATIONAL VEHICLES (RVS); SAILING; SLEIGHS; SNOWSHOES; WALKING.

Sports Cars

Sports cars are high-performance vehicles that can be used both for everyday driving and for racing. Smaller, sleeker, and lower to the ground than most passenger vehicles, sports cars often have room only for the driver and one passenger. What they lack in size, though, sports cars make up for in performance. They usually accelerate faster and handle better in turns than the average family car. Many also have convertible tops, which on warm, sunny days adds to the pleasure of driving them.

History. Sports cars appeared in Europe during the early 1900s, about the same time passenger cars were being developed there and in the United States. According to some historians, the 1903 Mercedes 60 ranks as the first sports car. From the beginning, sports cars were closely linked with automobiles built specially for racing. In 1910 the Alfa Romeo company was founded in Italy for the purpose of building both

Sports cars, such as this 1954 Jaguar convertible, feature high-performance engines that provide fast acceleration and good handling on curves.

race cars and sports cars. Enzo Ferrari, who developed the expensive, finely crafted Ferrari sports cars in the 1950s, also produced a series of prize-winning race cars.

Until the 1950s, European sports cars such as the MG, Triumph, Porsche, Jaguar, Aston Martin, and Ferrari dominated the market. The popularity of these automobiles led U.S. manufacturers to develop their own models. In 1953 General Motors introduced the Chevrolet Corvette, which became one of the most popular American sports cars. Soon other American automakers followed suit, including Ford with the Thunderbird. Japanese manufacturers have also produced sports cars.

Racing. Many sports car races are held in Europe and North America. In some races, production models—factory-built cars—are specially modified to enhance their performance. The two basic types of races for sports cars are rallies and road races. In rallies, drivers must follow a preset course over public roads and drive at prescribed speeds so that they pass through rally checkpoints at specific times. Regional sports car associations hold rallies for amateur drivers. Major international rallies—including one in Monte Carlo—bring together drivers from around the world.

In road races, sports cars compete on tracks consisting of irregular curves and straightaways, rather than a simple oval track. Some sports car events are endurance races that last for many hours. Challenging 24-hour endurance races are held at Le Mans, France; Sebring, Florida; Monza, Italy; and other locations. Another major international competition, the Trans-Am Championship, is a series of 100-mile (160-km) road races in the United States and Canada for modified production sports cars. *See also* AUTOMOBILE INDUSTRY; AUTOMOBILES, HISTORY OF; AUTOMOBILES, TYPES OF; CONVERTIBLES; RACE CARS.

Sport Utility Vehicles

A sport utility vehicle (SUV) is a heavy, oversized car mounted on a pickup truck frame. These four-wheel drive vehicles became popular in the 1990s as lower fuel prices rekindled the American love affair with big automobiles.

When an oil shortage caused gas prices to skyrocket in the mid-1970s, American automobiles began to lose market share to smaller, imported cars that were more fuel-efficient. However, by the 1990s, prices had come down and Americans began buying large automobiles again. Sport utility vehicles were favored by drivers who wanted powerful machines. Designed for off-road use, most sport utility vehicles are equipped with V-8 engines.

Many American and foreign automakers have developed SUV models. Among the popular types are the Ford Explorer and Jeep Grand Cherokee, but luxury car makers such as Mercedes-Benz and Cadillac also offer SUVs.

As more and more sport utility vehicles have appeared on streets and highways, various groups have raised environmental and safety concerns. Equipped with large engines, SUVs guzzle fuel and have poor gas mileage. Furthermore, these vehicles cause three times as much air pollution as cars do. They are classified as trucks and consequently do not have to meet the **emissions** standards imposed on passenger cars. In the late 1990s, some automakers voluntarily modified SUVs to conform to the low-emissions standards for cars. The Environmental Protection Agency (EPA) proposed regulations that would significantly reduce the amount of **pollutants** released by sport utility vehicles starting with the 2004 model year.

emissions *substances discharged into the air*

pollutant *something that contaminates the environment*

Originally designed for off-road use, most sport utility vehicles feature four-wheel drive that can handle rough terrain. The vehicle shown here travels along a dirt road in the Himalaya Mountains.

Concerns about the safety of SUVs arose from the fact that they stand much wider and higher than passenger cars, making it difficult for drivers riding behind them to see the traffic ahead. The vehicles' headlights are mounted higher, too, creating serious glare problems for automobiles with a lower profile. Finally, SUVs are more likely to roll over if they hit a curb, guardrail, or another vehicle. *See also* Automobile Industry; Automobiles, Effects of; Automobiles, History of.

Sputnik 1

Soviet Union *nation that existed from 1922 to 1991, made up of Russia and 14 other republics in eastern Europe and northern Asia*

On October 4, 1957, the **Soviet Union** launched *Sputnik 1*, the first artificial satellite to orbit the Earth. Not only was the launching a national triumph for the Soviet space program, but it also marked the beginning of the Space Age.

The Space Race. In the late 1920s, scientists and others interested in the possibility of space flight began to form rocket societies in the Soviet Union, Germany, the United States, and elsewhere. When World War II began, most of these groups became inactive as national attention shifted from the development of rocket technology to conventional weapons. Germany, however, continued to conduct research and test experimental rockets.

The end of the world war in 1945 marked the start of the Cold War, an era of competition and suspicion between the United States and the Soviet Union. The two nations used their space programs as a way to demonstrate their power. Building on the knowledge and achievements of German scientists, both countries made rapid progress in missile development in the early 1950s.

Soviet and American scientists and rocket engineers viewed the launch of artificial satellites into orbit around the Earth as an essential step toward human space flight. They pointed out that such satellites could perform many useful functions in communications and research. Both the United States and the Soviet Union developed plans to launch satellites using rockets. On October 4, 1957, American government and military leaders and scientists were unpleasantly surprised to learn that the Soviets had succeeded in putting a satellite into orbit—first.

Sputnik Successes. *Sputnik 1* (Russian for "traveling companion") was a steel globe that weighed 184 pounds (84 kg) and measured 23 inches (58 cm) across. Its four metal antennas broadcast radio signals back to Earth. Scientists and amateur radio operators all over the world tracked its progress by listening to the steady "beep, beep" it transmitted.

Sputnik 1 orbited the Earth once every 96 minutes, and its distance from the planet ranged from 142 miles (228 km) to 589 miles (948 km). Three months after it was launched, it fell out of orbit and burned up in the Earth's atmosphere. *Sputnik 1* was a tremendous success, proving that artificial satellites could function and drawing wide attention to space exploration. One of its most important effects was to stimulate new efforts in the U.S. space program. The U.S. Army succeeded in launching *Explorer 1,* the first American satellite, into orbit on January 31, 1958.

The Soviet Union continued its Sputnik satellite program between 1957 and 1961. *Sputnik 2* carried the first living creature—a dog named Laika—into space, and *Sputnik 3* was a large satellite that held a variety of scientific equipment and remained in orbit for almost two years. The Soviets launched a total of ten Sputniks, including some that paved the way for later piloted spaceflight, but none had the powerful emotional and political effects of *Sputnik 1. See also* ROCKETS; SATELLITES; SPACE EXPLORATION.

Stagecoaches

Movies and television programs set in the Old West usually show a stagecoach bouncing along a dusty road with anxious passengers, fearful of attack, peering out the windows. The use of stagecoaches, however, was not limited to the American frontier. These vehicles provided long-distance public transportation throughout Europe and the United States from the 1600s to the early 1900s.

Basic Design. A coach is a closed carriage built to hold passengers on facing seats, with the driver on a separate seat in front of the passenger cabin. Pulled by four or six horses, coaches traveled at speeds between 4 miles (6 km) and 10 miles (16 km) per hour, depending on the condition of the roads. Public coaches followed regular routes between inns or relay stations. Passengers traveled in stages or intervals from one stop to the next, leading to the term *stage travel.*

The crude suspension systems on early stagecoaches earned them a reputation for a bumpy ride. During the mid-1700s, carriage makers

Stagecoaches provided long-distance public transportation in Europe as early as the 1600s. The stagecoach in this photograph was traveling across South Dakota in 1889.

introduced metal springs to make travel more comfortable. Over time passenger travel on stagecoaches improved with advances in manufacturing methods and smoother road surfaces.

Use and Development. Upper-class Europeans traveled around in a version of the coach as early as the 1450s. But it was not until the 1600s that coaches came to be used as a form of public transportation between towns. By about 1670 a stagecoach service was operating between London, England, and Edinburgh, Scotland—a distance of 392 miles (631 km). During the 1750s public lines were established in colonial America, running from Boston, Philadelphia, and New York to nearby destinations. Many of the stagecoaches were actually wagons with benches. Passengers called them "Shake Guts" because of the jolting ride.

Stagecoaches received a huge boost from the new American government in 1785, when its Congress decided that the post office should send mail by coach rather than by horse and rider. Mail carrying became the stagecoach companies' chief source of income. However, passenger travel also increased as stage lines moved westward into new territories.

In the early 1800s, J. Stephen Abbot and Lewis Downing of Concord, New Hampshire, introduced a new type of stagecoach. Lightweight and well-made, the Concord coach featured an oval body, flat roof, luggage racks, and a high driver's seat. With doors on both sides, it could seat between 6 and 16 passengers. The coach had rear wheels that were 5 feet (1.5 m) high and front wheels that were just under 4 feet (1 m) high, which provided balance and improved steering capability. The exterior was decorated with paintings of landscapes or actresses.

Concord coaches soon became the primary form of cross-country public transportation on the nation's roads. Other popular stagecoaches included the Troy coach, manufactured in Troy, New York, and the mud wagon, a lightweight vehicle with narrow tires to prevent it from sinking into muddy trails.

The use of the stagecoach for passenger and mail travel began to decrease in the United States with the building of the railroads during the mid-1800s. Most companies dedicated to long-distance stage service were out of business by the 1880s. Still, coaches continued to carry passengers to railroad lines, and Concord coaches provided service between hotels and railroad stations. In the west, stagecoaches remained in use until the 1920s when the autobus began to appear on roads. *See also* CARTS, CARRIAGES, AND WAGONS; PONY EXPRESS.

Standard Time Zones

In the late 1880s most nations adopted a system of standard time zones, making the measurement of time across the globe consistent. The system allows people to calculate exactly what time it is in any place in the world and to coordinate travel and communications in different regions.

History of the Zone System. Before the introduction of railroads and the telegraph in the mid-1800s, travel was slow. As a result,

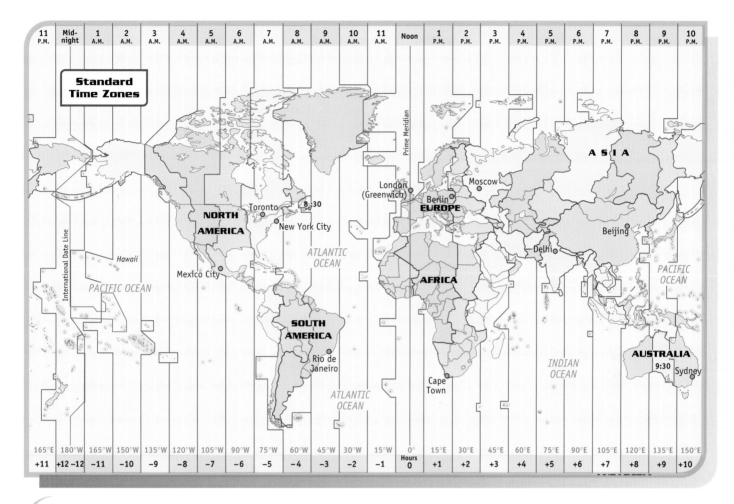

11 P.M.	Mid-night	1 A.M.	2 A.M.	3 A.M.	4 A.M.	5 A.M.	6 A.M.	7 A.M.	8 A.M.	9 A.M.	10 A.M.	11 A.M.	Noon	1 P.M.	2 P.M.	3 P.M.	4 P.M.	5 P.M.	6 P.M.	7 P.M.	8 P.M.	9 P.M.	10 P.M.

Standard Time Zones

165°E	180°W	165°W	150°W	135°W	120°W	105°W	90°W	75°W	60°W	45°W	30°W	15°W	0° Hours	15°E	30°E	45°E	60°E	75°E	90°E	105°E	120°E	135°E	150°E
+11	+12 –12	–11	–10	–9	–8	–7	–6	–5	–4	–3	–2	–1	0	+1	+2	+3	+4	+5	+6	+7	+8	+9	+10

The standard time zone system makes it possible to calculate the exact time in any place in the world.

longitude *distance east or west of the prime meridian, an imaginary line on the Earth's surface that runs through Greenwich, England*

the variations in time between one location and another did not seem to matter. However, the growth of faster methods of transportation and communications greatly increased exchanges between people from different regions, creating the need for a uniform time system.

Great Britain established a measure of standard time for England, Scotland, and Wales in 1850. In 1883 U.S. railroads approved a system of four time zones for the continental United States. The following year representatives from many nations met in Washington, D.C., to discuss plans for a world system of standard time zones. They chose Greenwich, England, as the prime meridian—the line of **longitude** that serves as the starting point for measuring time. Most nations eventually adopted the standard time zones proposed at the conference.

How Time Zones Work. The world is divided into 24 time zones, each representing an hour in the Earth's day-and-night cycle. The zones run north to south between the poles, and each covers 15 degrees of longitude. Many countries have multiple time zones. The United States contains six time zones—the Eastern, Central, Mountain, Pacific, Alaska, and Hawaiian-Aleutian—that extend from east to west. An additional zone, the Atlantic, covers the U.S. Virgin Islands and Puerto Rico.

The system's starting point is Greenwich Mean Time (GMT), the zone that includes Greenwich, England. GMT is considered 0 hours.

Time zones east of Greenwich are ahead of GMT and are termed +1, +2, and so on. Time zones west of Greenwich are behind GMT and are termed –1, –2, and so on. Two people traveling in opposite directions from Greenwich would meet at the international date line, which lies between the +12 and –12 zones in the Pacific Ocean. The date line is the point at which one day becomes another.

In theory the time in each zone should coordinate with the line of longitude that runs through it. In reality, however, zone boundaries may vary to keep states and countries within a single time zone. Even the international date line zigzags so that it will always be the same day in the Aleutian Islands as in neighboring Alaska. *See also* LATITUDE AND LONGITUDE.

Stars

see Navigation.

Steamboats

tributary *stream or river that flows into a larger stream or river*

Robert Fulton's steamboat, the Clermont, began commercial service on the Hudson River between Albany and New York City in 1807. The boat had paddle wheels, mounted on either side of the hull, that turned in the water to move the boat forward.

Although a steamboat may be defined as any watercraft powered by steam, the term is generally associated with the paddle wheel steamboats that flourished on the Mississippi River and its **tributaries** during the 1800s. Steamboats carried much of the passenger and cargo traffic on American rivers until railroads were built along those waterways toward the end of the century.

Early Steamboats and Development. In 1807 the *Clermont,* Robert Fulton's steamboat, began commercial service on the Hudson River between New York City and Albany. The vessel completed the one-way journey in just 32 hours, a significant improvement over the four-day voyage on a sailing ship and a key to the steamboat's success.

The *Clermont* had a narrow wooden hull that measured 133 feet (41 m) long. Equipped with a 20-horsepower steam engine that could burn both wood and coal, the *Clermont* cruised at a speed of 5 miles per hour (8 km per hour). Mounted on either side of the hull were 15-foot (5-m) wheels. These were connected to paddles that turned in the water, moving the boat forward.

In the following years, steamboats began appearing on waterways up and down the East Coast. Among the early vessels was the *Phoenix,* which provided regular service on the Delaware River. By 1811 to 1812 the *New Orleans*—another of Fulton's steamboats—managed to navigate the waterways from Pittsburgh south to New Orleans. Several years later steamboat service was started on the Great Lakes.

Riverboats and Steamships. The basic model of the riverboat was built in 1816 by Henry Miller Shreve. Designed to navigate the shallow waters of the Mississippi, the *Washington* featured a broad, flat bottom. It was propelled by two side-mounted paddle wheels, each operated by a separate high-pressure steam engine for generating speed upstream. Featuring two tall smokestacks and three decks, the *Washington* became the standard design for a whole generation of Mississippi steamboats that followed it.

By 1819 more than 60 steamboats traveled the Mississippi, Missouri, and Ohio Rivers. As their numbers increased and as steamboat service expanded, these vessels played an important role in the settlement of the western United States. In 1860 a steamboat pushed as far west as Fort Benton, Montana. The craft used on western rivers, such as the Missouri and the Colorado, generally featured rear-mounted paddle wheels that could be raised to avoid obstacles in shallow waters. Rear-mounted wheels also allowed more room for cargo.

Meanwhile, large seaworthy steamboats began transporting freight and passengers on coastal routes along the Atlantic Ocean. In 1819 a steamboat designed for oceangoing service, the *Savannah,* completed the first **transatlantic** journey in 29 days. However, the vessel had to use both steam and sail power because it could not store enough fuel for the entire trip.

By the mid-1800s, steamship lines offered regular service across the Atlantic. Instead of paddle wheels, the vessels that sailed the open seas were equipped with screw propellers. The propeller provided the power needed to sail in rough waters, where side-mounted paddle wheels did not perform well. Later designs replaced the propellers with steam turbines and substituted oil for coal and wood. Steamships also featured iron hulls instead of wooden ones, eventually switching to steel. Most transatlantic steamship lines were run by Europeans. American steamship owners focused on the development of inland and coastal water routes.

transatlantic *relating to crossing the Atlantic Ocean*

Height and Decline of Steamboats. Large, luxurious riverboats went into service on the Mississippi and other major American rivers in the years following the Civil War. Floating palaces like the *Robert E. Lee* and the *Natchez* transported goods such as cotton and sugar. Passengers enjoyed elaborately decorated cabins as well as dining, drinking, and gambling in the main saloon. But during the 1870s, competition from railroads, which had built lines alongside the rivers, steadily drew business away from the steamboats. By the early 1900s steamboats had all but disappeared from American waterways. Today paddle wheel steamers are used as pleasure boats. *See also* ENGINES; FULTON, ROBERT; RIVERS OF THE WORLD; SHIPS AND BOATS.

Steam Engine

see Engines.

Stephenson, George
British inventor

During George Stephenson's lifelong career in the mining industry, he sought to improve the transportation of coal from the mines. His work with steam locomotives led to the founding of the modern railway.

Born in 1781, George Stephenson became an assistant in a coal mine at Newcastle, England, at the age of 14. When Stephenson entered the mining industry, mines used horses to pull the coal-filled wagons along tracks called tramlines. By the early 1800s, Stephenson began experimenting

George Stephenson works on a model of his Rocket locomotive. This invention played a key role in the development of rail transportation in Europe and the United States.

with steam engines to power cars on the lines. With the financial backing of the mining industry, Stephenson built lines linking several coal mines and began developing steam locomotives.

In 1826 Stephenson became engineer of the Liverpool and Manchester Railway line. Together with his son Robert, he developed a locomotive called the *Rocket* that outperformed other locomotives in a competition held in 1829. The Liverpool-Manchester line officially opened the following year. It was the first railway that used only locomotives to pull cars, marking the beginning of the modern age of railways.

Stephenson's success with the *Rocket* made him famous. He helped develop northern England's railway network, and he founded the Institution of Mechanical Engineers in 1847. Stephenson died the following year. *See also* RAILROADS, HISTORY OF.

Streetcars

see Light Rail Systems.

Submarines and Submersibles

Submarines are ships that can cruise underwater for long periods. They play a significant role in naval operations. Submersibles are smaller craft used for underwater research, rescue, and **salvage**. Some submersibles can dive as deep as 20,000 feet (6,100 m), well beyond the range of submarines.

salvage saving or recovering property lost underwater

maneuver to make a series of changes in course

History of Submarines

Inventors have worked on developing deep-sea vessels for centuries. The task involves several challenges, including creating a watertight craft, **maneuvering** underwater, supplying air for the crew, and designing suitable engines.

Early Designs. The first known voyage of an underwater craft occurred in 1620 on the Thames River in England. This crude submarine, built by a Dutchman named Cornelius van Drebbel, was a 12-passenger wooden rowboat covered with leather. The oars protruded through waterproof seals in the leather, and the craft could cruise at a depth of 15 feet (5 m) for several hours.

The first military submarine, the *Turtle,* was built in 1775 by Connecticut inventor David Bushnell. Robert Fulton's copper-hulled *Nautilus,* completed in 1800, introduced diving planes—horizontal wings that help subs dive and surface. The *Nautilus* included a supply of compressed air for crew members to breathe, which extended the time they could remain underwater.

During the Civil War, a Confederate submarine, the *Hunley,* became the first sub to actually sink a ship. Carrying an explosive charge at the end of a 10-foot (3-m) beam, the iron-hulled *Hunley* succeeded in ramming the *Housatonic,* a Union warship. The resulting explosion sent both ships to the bottom.

Parts of a Nuclear Submarine

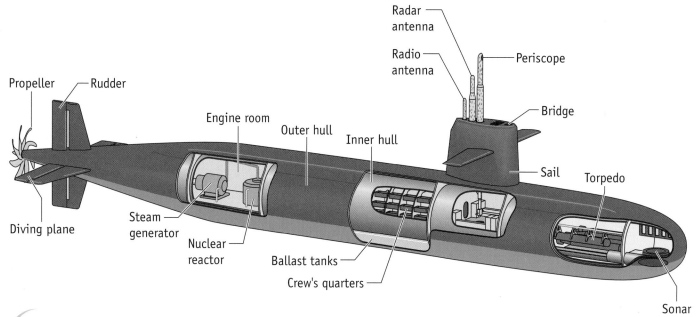

Propeller — Rudder

Engine room

Outer hull

Inner hull

Radar antenna

Radio antenna

Periscope

Bridge

Sail

Torpedo

Diving plane

Steam generator

Nuclear reactor

Ballast tanks

Crew's quarters

Sonar

The design of submarines allows them to travel underwater for long periods.

propulsion *process of driving or propelling*

knot *unit of measure of a ship's speed, equal to about 1.15 miles (1.85 km) per hour*

The first practical submarine built by the American inventor John Holland in 1898 combined a gasoline engine for surface **propulsion** with battery-powered electric motors for use underwater. Known as the *Holland,* it was the first submarine purchased by the U.S. Navy. It had a steel hull and a torpedo tube and could cruise at 7 **knots** down to a depth of 75 feet (23 m).

Several improvements occurred in submarine design in the early 1900s. Safer and more efficient diesel engines replaced gasoline engines for surface cruising. Designers also added a periscope, a tube-shaped instrument for viewing objects above the water.

Wartime Role. World War I saw the first extensive use of submarines in combat. German submarines, known as U-boats, took a terrible toll on both unarmed merchant vessels and warships of the Allied powers. U-boats sank more than 6,000 ships in the Atlantic Ocean during the war.

During World War II larger, faster subs armed with improved, highly accurate torpedoes threatened ships in both the Atlantic and Pacific Oceans. Early in the war, German U-boats attacked Allied vessels in the Atlantic, including many carrying vital supplies from the United States to Britain. By the war's end, U-boats had managed to sink more than 3,500 vessels. Meanwhile, U.S. submarines destroyed about 200 Japanese warships and 1,200 cargo vessels in the Pacific. Eventually, ships began traveling in **convoys** and using **sonar** to detect submarines in the water.

convoy *group of ships, aircraft, or land vehicles that travel together for security and convenience*

sonar *short for sound navigation and ranging; system that uses sound waves to locate underwater objects*

Nuclear Submarines. The two world wars demonstrated the submarine's strengths, and an important weakness—the need to surface periodically to take on fresh air and recharge batteries. In fact, submarines were really surface vessels that could submerge.

The first nuclear submarine, built in 1954, was a ship designed to operate under the water's surface rather than on it. The new submarine, the U.S. Navy's *Nautilus,* was powered by a small nuclear reactor that produced steam to drive the sub's steam turbine engines. The 319-foot (97-m) vessel cruised at more than 20 knots and could stay underwater for months at a time.

Nuclear submarines opened up new possibilities for scientific research and military activity. In 1958 the *Nautilus* made history when it completed the first voyage under the north polar icecap. Two years later the USS *Triton* cruised all the way around the world without surfacing.

In 1960 the U.S. Navy created a new class of submarines armed with ballistic missiles that could destroy cities and other targets thousands of miles away. Because submarines are difficult to track, they became a vital strategic weapon for both the United States and the **Soviet Union** during the **Cold War.** The U.S. Navy operates both attack submarines, designed to locate and bombard enemy ships and subs, and ballistic missile submarines, which carry long-distance missiles. The Navy groups submarines of a similar size and design into classes, such as the Seawolf, Virginia, Los Angeles, or Ohio class.

Soviet Union nation that existed from 1922 to 1991, made up of Russia and 14 other republics in eastern Europe and northern Asia

Cold War period of tense relations between the United States and the Soviet Union following World War II

The First Combat Sub

In August 1776, during the American Revolution, the *Turtle* became the first submarine ever used in combat. Continental Army sergeant Ezra Lee set out at night in the crude one-person sub to sink the *Eagle,* a British flagship moored off Manhattan.

Lee maneuvered the sub under the *Eagle* and began turning a screw mechanism to bore through the ship's copper sheathing. His plan was to screw a mine onto the wooden hull. But Lee had unwittingly positioned the sub under some iron straps on the hull, and the screw mechanism could not pierce them. Abandoning the attempt, he cast the mine into the water and returned to safety. The mine drifted away from the *Eagle* and later exploded, causing no damage.

Design and Operation

The design of submarines allows them to dive and resurface, travel underwater, and remain submerged for long periods. Navigating beneath the waves, without a view of the surroundings on the surface, requires precise information and carefully planned maneuvers.

Submarine Design. The submarine's hull must be able to withstand tremendous pressure. When a sub dives, the force of the water pressure increases sharply. Most subs are designed with a double hull. The inner one, which contains the engines and the crew's quarters, is reinforced to protect crew members and equipment from the pressure of the deep sea. The space between the two hulls holds items that are not affected by water pressure, such as fuel tanks. The hull's rounded, streamlined shape allows the submarine to move through the water easily.

The sail—a tall, thin structure rising from the top of the hull—houses the periscope, radar, and radio antennae. It also includes an observation platform, called the bridge, that the captain and crew use when the sub is running on the surface.

Submarine Maneuvers. Submarines move through the water in much the same way airplanes fly through the air. They can go up or down and from side to side. One or two propellers at the submarine's stern drive the craft forward or backward in the water. A vertical rudder steers the submarine left or right. Horizontal diving planes, located at the stern and toward the bow, help the submarine surface or plunge.

To make a submarine dive, the crew lets seawater flow into tanks in the outer hull. The water acts as ballast, material used to increase the

buoyancy force that exerts an upward push on an object

ship's weight and change its **buoyancy** so it will no longer float on the surface. The crew also angles the diving planes toward the bottom. Water passing over the diving planes provides a strong downward push.

Resurfacing involves the reverse procedure. Compressed air enters the ballast tanks, forcing the seawater out. This lightens the sub and restores its buoyancy, and it begins to rise. With the diving planes angled upward, the sub tilts toward the surface.

Underwater Operation. Once a submarine submerges, it is effectively cut off from the outside world. It can receive low-frequency radio signals but can only send messages when near the surface by raising an antenna out of the water. Though living and working areas are cramped, crews aboard nuclear submarines have everything they need to stay submerged for months at a time. Special equipment produces oxygen and freshwater from seawater. Because there are no viewing

As this military submarine rises to the surface, the observation platform and communication antennae become visible.

ports on submarines, the captain relies on sonar equipment to "see" any obstacles that lie ahead in the water. Sonar is also used to locate and track nearby ships.

Submarines are equipped with inertial guidance systems, devices that monitor changes in speed and direction to keep the vessel on course. Satellite navigation systems, such as global positioning systems, help determine the sub's position. When cruising close to the surface, the captain can scan the surrounding area through the periscope.

In war submarines may be used to attack other submarines, surface ships, or even targets on land. Most U.S. subs are equipped to carry both torpedoes and missiles to fire on ships and land targets. Subs that carry ballistic missiles, such as the Trident II, can strike locations thousands of miles away.

Propulsion System. Before the introduction of nuclear power, submarines had two propulsion systems: diesel engines for surface running and battery-powered electric motors for cruising underwater. Both were connected to a driveshaft that turned the sub's propellers.

Electric motors were used underwater because, unlike diesel engines, they consumed no oxygen and released no toxic exhaust into the cabin. But relying on batteries severely limited the submarine's range, forcing it to surface periodically to recharge the batteries by running the diesel engine. During this time subs were visible to other ships and aircraft, which was a problem during combat missions.

Nuclear propulsion systems eliminated the need for periodic surfacing. Like electric motors, they do not release any exhaust. Energy generated by the nuclear reactor heats water that flows into a steam generator. The generator produces steam to drive the submarine's turbine engines. Nuclear submarines can run for years without refueling.

Submersibles

Before the development of submersibles, very little was known about the deep waters of the world's oceans. Submarines and other diving apparatus of the early 1900s could go no deeper than a few hundred feet. However, because the average depth of the oceans is about 12,000 feet (3,660 m), much territory remained to be explored.

In the 1950s the Swiss scientist Auguste Piccard built the first practical submersible for deepwater exploration. Scientists rode inside a heavy, thick-walled sphere with viewing ports that could withstand the pressure of water thousands of feet down. The sphere was suspended from large floats filled with gasoline, which was lighter than water so that it made the heavy craft buoyant. The *Trieste,* Piccard's most famous submersible, set a world record in 1960 by diving 35,800 feet (10,900 m) into the Marianas Trench, a deep canyon in the Pacific Ocean floor.

Since then many other submersibles have been built for underwater research and search-and-rescue operations. Scientists at Woods Hole Oceanographic Institute in Massachusetts can reach depths of about

14,800 feet (4,500 m) in a submersible called *Alvin.* The U.S. Navy operates the atomic-powered *NR-1* Deep Submergence Craft. It can carry a ten-person crew 20,000 feet (6,100 m) or more below the surface. The Navy also maintains Deep Submergence Rescue Vehicles (DSRVs) for use in emergencies involving submarines. DSRVs, which attach directly to the stricken submarine's escape hatch, can bring 24 crew members to the surface at a time. *See also* BALLAST; CONVOYS; DIVING; FULTON, ROBERT; GLOBAL POSITIONING SYSTEM (GPS); GUIDED MISSILES; NAVIES; NAVIGATION; RADAR; SALVAGE; SONAR.

Subways

Many of the world's largest cities have underground railway systems called subways. Also known as the underground, tube, or metro, subways are one of the most important forms of urban mass transit. They offer transportation in urban areas without the delays and frustrations of motor vehicle traffic.

Subway trains consist of connected sets of cars that run on a network of tracks. Passengers board the trains at stations along a route, or line. For the most part, subway systems operate underground, but outlying sections sometimes run on surface-level or elevated tracks. Subway passengers may have the opportunity to transfer to other forms of urban transportation, such as buses and light rail systems, at certain points.

History of Subways. The growth of cities in the 1800s coincided with the development of railroads. The idea of an underground railway for urban transportation was first presented in London in 1843. After more than a decade of planning, work began in 1860. The first portion of London's subway was completed three years later. Called the Underground or Tube, it ran for 3.75 miles (6 km) beneath the city streets.

The cars of London's Underground were pulled by steam-powered locomotives, which filled the tunnels with smoke. Nonetheless, the Underground carried almost 10 million passengers during its first year of operation. Its success led to the construction of additional lines in London, including the world's first electric-powered subway, which opened in 1890.

The use of electricity eliminated the problem of smoky tunnels and encouraged the construction of subway systems in other major cities around the world. In Paris an 8.7-mile (14-km) subway line opened in 1900. The Paris subway became known as the Métropolitain or Métro.

In the United States, the first successful subway was built in Boston between 1895 and 1897. The line was 1.5 miles (2.4 km) long and used electric-powered trolley cars. New York City opened its first subway in 1904. By the late 1990s, its subway system consisted of about 842 miles (1,355 km) of track and 468 stations and carried more than one billion passengers a year.

Early subway lines were built and managed by private transit companies. By the mid-1900s, however, most systems were owned and operated by government-controlled transit companies or public agencies. Because subway lines are very expensive to build, cities rely heavily on government funding and support.

Updating the Paris Métro

In 1998 a new, completely automated line called the Météor opened in the Paris Métro. Its trains have no driver or conductor and speed along at more than 50 miles (80 km) per hour. At stations, a transparent plastic barrier separates passengers from the tracks, allowing people to see approaching trains but preventing them from falling on the tracks. When a train pulls in, doors on the cars and in the plastic barrier open simultaneously, allowing passengers to get on or off. Remote-controlled cameras monitor the station and the trains.

The world's first underground train opened in London in 1863 with less than 4 miles of track. The city's modern system has more than 250 stations and electric subway trains.

Design and Construction. Subway construction can be difficult and costly. Ground level and elevated portions of subway lines resemble traditional railroads and light rail systems. Underground portions, however, have various features that require special design and construction techniques.

There are several methods of building underground subway lines. In the open-cut method, workers tear out existing streets and dig deep trenches below street level. A variation of this approach involves laying a temporary roadway over the ditches to allow motor vehicle traffic to pass through the area while work proceeds on the subway lines below. New, permanent roadways are eventually constructed over the completed lines.

Another method is to tunnel deep within the earth. Although tunneling does not disturb the surface, it requires special engineering techniques for the different types of soil, rock, and underground conditions encountered during construction.

The work of building subways is complicated by various factors. Beneath the streets of major cities are countless miles of water pipes, sewers, and telephone and electrical lines. During subway construction these complex networks must be avoided, moved, or replaced. The underground foundations of large buildings nearby also must be taken into account while laying a subway line. Workers often install special support systems to stabilize and strengthen the foundations of such structures.

Subways require ventilation systems to remove stale air from underground tunnels and stations and to bring in fresh air from above ground. These systems consist of many large intake and exhaust fans, air filters, and air ducts. The air ducts serve as pathways for circulating air and provide a release for the strong winds caused by the passing of speeding trains.

Operation of Subways. Most modern subways are powered by electricity provided by a third rail located outside the running rails. Devices on the undersides of subway cars make contact with the third rail and transfer the electric current to the cars. On a few subway systems, electric lines run overhead.

Each car on a modern subway train has its own motor and controls, allowing the operator to control the entire train from a single car. The cars can also reverse direction at the end of a route instead of having to turn around.

Subway cars usually have metal wheels that run on steel rails similar to those used on a conventional railroad. Some subways, however, feature rubber tires that run on concrete tracks; small guide-wheels help keep the tires on the track. Rubber tires provide a smoother and quieter ride than metal wheels, but concrete tracks are complicated and expensive to build.

Signals and switches for directing the movements of subway trains are controlled by a traffic center. Computer displays show the track layout as well as the positions of all trains and the status of signals and switches in the system. Efficient signaling is extremely important, because many trains may be running through the system at the same time.

Subways have become highly automated, with computers operating subway cars, controlling all signals and switching, and monitoring train speeds and schedules. An attendant accompanies the train in case of emergency. The first completely automatic subway system in the United States was San Francisco's BART (Bay Area Rapid Transit) system, which opened in 1976. *See also* BART (BAY AREA RAPID TRANSIT); COMMUTING; GOVERNMENT AND TRANSPORTATION; LIGHT RAIL SYSTEMS; PUBLIC TRANSPORTATION; TUNNELS; URBAN TRANSPORTATION.

Suez Canal

The Suez Canal is a 101-mile (163-km) waterway that runs through the Egyptian desert, connecting the Mediterranean and Red Seas. The canal provides the quickest route for ships traveling between Europe and Asia, eliminating the long voyage around the southern tip of Africa.

Ancient Egyptians had dug a narrow canal from the Nile River east to the Red Sea by about 1900 B.C., but it eventually became unusable. Rebuilt and destroyed several times over the centuries, the canal was finally abandoned in the A.D. 700s.

In 1859 the Egyptian government granted a former French diplomat named Ferdinand de Lesseps the right to build a new canal. Despite technical, political, and financial problems during construction, the Suez Canal opened ten years later in 1869. Initially it was operated under joint French and Egyptian control; by 1875 the British had bought the Egyptian share in the canal company.

The canal was closed twice. In 1956 Egyptian President Gamal Abdel Nasser seized control of the waterway, and the resulting conflict with Great Britain and France prevented ships from traveling the Suez until the beginning of 1957. Later an Arab-Israeli War halted traffic on the canal from 1967 until 1975.

The Suez Canal begins at Port Said on the Mediterranean Sea and ends at the city of Suez on the Red Sea. Because the lakes it passes through and the seas it connects all lie at about the same level, no locks are required on the canal. The average time for a ship to pass through is 14 hours.

Until 1967, the Suez Canal was the busiest interocean waterway in the world, with an average of 58 passages per day. However, when operations were halted in 1967, tankers and other ships were forced to use alternate routes to reach their markets. In the 1990s the principal cargoes carried on the canal were grain, ores, and metals. *See also* CANALS; ERIE CANAL; LESSEPS, FERDINAND DE; PANAMA CANAL.

Supersonic Flight

maneuver to make a series of changes in course

Supersonic flight occurs when an aircraft travels faster than the speed of sound—about 760 miles per hour (1,223 km per hour) at sea level or 660 miles per hour (1,062 km per hour) at an altitude of 37,000 feet (11,278 m). Supersonic planes are specially designed to operate at such high speeds.

When a plane is flying, it creates pressure waves that push the air in its path out of the way. As the aircraft approaches the speed of sound, the pressure waves build up to form shock waves. The flow of air that would normally move the plane forward slows down. The craft experiences turbulence and begins to descend. **Maneuvering** the plane becomes difficult, increasing the risk that it will stall and lose power.

Most early jet planes were not powerful enough to reach the speed of sound. Those that attempted to do so could not withstand the severe forces created by shock waves, and many of them were torn apart before they could achieve supersonic flight. In 1943 American engineers began experimenting with rocket-driven planes that could break the "sound barrier." Four years later Charles E. Yeager, a U.S. Air Force captain, made the first supersonic flight in a Bell X-1 rocket plane. In the 1950s engineers designed jet engines that could reach supersonic speeds. The Concorde, a British-French supersonic transport plane, began passenger service in 1976. Travel time on the Concorde is about 3 hours and 33 minutes between Washington, D.C., and Paris—half that of a typical airliner.

Supersonic planes are designed to minimize shock waves. Some models feature wings that are swept backward, which decreases the speed at which air flows over the wing and increases the speed needed to produce shock waves. Others have wings with the same shape on both the top and bottom and a sharp leading, or front, edge. This design produces shock waves both in front of and behind the plane. As the plane reaches the speed of sound, the front shock wave moves back until it meets the trailing wave. This stabilizes the wave pattern and results in a smoother flight. *See also* CONCORDE; FLIGHT; JET PLANES; YEAGER, CHARLES.

Superstition at Sea

ritual ceremonial act

Superstition is a form of belief in forces that control or influence events in the world. Many superstitions are concerned with fortune or luck—attracting good luck and avoiding bad luck. Superstitions are often dismissed as foolish or ignorant. But some superstitious beliefs, such as a few notions about predicting the weather, are founded on a grain of good sense. Logical or not, traditions have a way of lingering in people's minds and customs.

Various forms of transportation have acquired traditions, but none has had more superstitious beliefs associated with it than sailing. Whole books have been written about the folklore and superstitions of the sea. Such beliefs cover all aspects of seafaring, from shipbuilding to burial at sea.

Some superstitions connected with ships can be traced to **rituals** that shipbuilders performed to protect the vessels. New ships were launched with elaborate naming ceremonies. Sailors considered it unlucky to change the name later. Many sailing ships had figureheads—carved wooden figures with large, staring eyes—attached to their bows. Often impressive works of art, figureheads were descended from the *oculus,* an image of an "all-seeing" eye that ancient peoples such as the Phoenicians and Romans thought could protect a ship from evil spirits.

Many sailors' superstitions and traditional beliefs centered on weather, upon which their lives depended. People today still hold some of these age-old beliefs, such as that a ring around the moon means that rain or snow is on the way. A well-known rhyme gives an old sailors' method of forecasting weather:

> Red sky at morning,
> Sailors take warning.
> Red sky at night,
> Sailors delight.

See also LITERATURE; SONGS.

Swimming

see Sports and Recreation.

Tankers

A tanker is a ship designed to transport liquid cargo. Most tankers carry oil, but some haul other liquids—such as wine and molasses—or various dry materials. Modern supertankers that can hold hundreds of thousands of tons of oil are the largest ships ever built.

History of Tankers. Before the late 1800s, oil was transported in barrels aboard regular cargo ships. The first vessel designed as a tanker was the German *Glückauf,* built in 1886. Oil was stored in chambers in the hull of the ship. Within 15 years, such tankers carried 99 percent of the oil shipped by sea.

Early tankers usually hauled no more than a few thousand tons of oil. However, in 1912 the British Navy decided to switch from coal to oil as the main fuel for its warships. Tankers up to 15,000 tons were built to transport larger quantities of oil. During the mid-1900s the worldwide demand for oil continued to increase and even larger tankers were constructed.

By the 1970s, very large crude carriers (VLCCs) appeared that measured more than 1,000 feet (305 m) long and 150 feet (46 m) wide, extended 60 feet (18 m) below the surface of the water, and carried some 275,000 tons of oil. The biggest tankers today are almost 1½ times as large and hold more than twice as much oil.

Tanker Design. Tankers are basically floating oil tanks propelled by an engine. Instead of having a single tank, the hull is divided into a series of compartments to reduce the movement of oil caused by the swaying of the ship. Oil is pumped into the tanks through a system of pipes and unloaded by reversing the direction of the pumps. Heating coils in the tanks warm the oil in cold climates to make pumping easier.

Tankers are designed to transport liquid cargo. Supertankers, such as the one seen in this photo, can hold around 250,000 tons of oil and are the largest ships ever built.

EXXON NORTH SLOPE

maneuver series of changes in course

facilities something built or created to serve a particular function

The rest of the ship consists of an engine room and a building at the stern called a superstructure, which houses the bridge and crew quarters.

Tankers are easy to operate because they have a very simple design and generally travel in a straight line at a constant speed. As a result, they need a relatively small crew, which makes them inexpensive to use. In fact, as a tanker's size increases, the cost of transporting each gallon of oil decreases.

There are several drawbacks to the tanker's dimensions and design. Its great size prevents it from performing complex **maneuvers.** Even in an emergency, a tanker may take up to 3 miles (5 km) to come to a complete stop. Some tankers cannot sail in water that is less than 80 feet (24 m) deep, but most harbor channels are only about 50 feet (15 m) deep. For this reason, tankers may require special offshore loading and unloading **facilities.**

A tanker's design also limits the type of cargo it can carry. Because countries that import oil usually do not also export it, a tanker must often make its return trip empty except for ballast—water pumped into the tanks to stabilize the ship.

Other Types of Tankers.

Some tankers are built to carry ore or other dry materials, rather than oil. Dry cargo is often mixed with water to form a slurry that can be pumped into and out of the tanks. Solid cargo can also be loaded into the tanks through hatches in the deck of the ship. Some tankers are designed to transport both oil and dry cargo, which allows them to reload with another cargo after delivering a load of oil.

A special kind of tanker is used to carry natural gas. The gas is chilled so that it shrinks to a fraction of its normal size and turns into a liquid. It is stored in insulated tanks made of aluminum because the very cold liquid would make steel tanks too brittle.

Environmental Concerns.

Accidents involving tankers often result in oil spills that pollute the water. In 1989 the *Exxon Valdez* ran aground off the shore of Alaska, releasing almost 37,000 tons of oil. It is estimated that more than a million tons of oil are spilled each year as a result of tanker accidents. Precautions such as the use of double hulls can prevent oil from flowing out of a disabled tanker. *See also* BALLAST; CARGO SHIPS; FREIGHT; HARBORS AND PORTS; SHIPPING INDUSTRY; SHIPS AND BOATS, TYPES OF.

Index

Index